Lord, I Love the Church and We Need Help

"Lord! I love the church! She is that magnificent place where you stand in the gap between your kingdom in heaven and your kingdom on earth!" Those stirring words capture the passion and insight that Dr. Bassford brings to the discussion of the life of the Church. Built on the concept of relationships and why they matter, Dr. Bassford both invites and challenges us to step into a new, vibrant future led by the Lord. Pastors and lay leaders will be blessed by the cogent sharing of the best of contemporary leadership insight with deep spirituality. Relationships are the key, and the Lord offers us the help we need. This deep insight is illustrated in a down-to-earth style that is readily applicable to churches of all sizes.

—Mike Lowry, Resident Bishop of the Central Texas Conference, The United Methodist Church

Lord, I do love the Church and we do need your help! Pastor, teacher, DS, and fellow pilgrim Virginia Bassford has offered all of us who cherish the Church a living prayer of hope. Aflame with inspiring stories and hard-won wisdom, this book is for all who long for renewal and trust God's good news to yet fill our pews.

—Craig T. Kocher, University Chaplain and Jessie Ball duPont Chair of the Chaplaincy, University of Richmond, and United Methodist Minister

Many leaders in our church speak as though the church is dead and buried, beyond resuscitation and even resurrection. Dr. Bassford reminds us in striking terms that not only is the church *not* dead, it has as much potential as ever. This book is a clarion call to return to a clear understanding of our identity and purpose as the incarnate body of Christ, seeking and serving the Will of God in all we say and do. If we love the church and trust in God's power, the time to act is now!

—Dan R. Dick, Director of Connectional Ministries, Wisconsin Annual Conference

ADAPTIVE LEADERSHIP SERIES

Lord
I love the Church
and We need
Help

Virginia O. Bassford

Abingdon Press
Nashville

LORD, I LOVE THE CHURCH AND WE NEED HELP

Copyright © 2012 by Abingdon Press

This book is printed on acid-free paper.

Library of Congress Cataloging-in-Publication Data

Bassford, Virginia O.
  Lord, I love the church and we need help / Virginia O. Bassford.
    p. cm.
  Includes bibliographical references (p.).
  ISBN 978-1-4267-4040-4 (book - pbk. / trade pbk. : alk. paper)
  1. Pastoral theology—United Methodist Church (U.S.) 2. Church work—United Methodist Church (U.S.) I. Title.
  BV4011.3.B38 2012
  253—dc23

                                                                    2011041511

All Scripture quotations, unless noted otherwise, are taken from the New Revised Standard Version of the Bible, copyright 1989, Division of Christian Education of the National Council of the Churches of Christ in the United States of America. Used by permission. All rights reserved.

Scripture quotations marked RSV are taken from the Revised Standard Version of the Bible, copyright 1952 [2nd edition, 1971] by the Division of Christian Education of the National Council of the Churches of Christ in the United States of America. Used by permission. All rights reserved.

12 13 14 15 16 17 18 19 20 21—10 9 8 7 6 5 4 3 2 1
MANUFACTURED IN THE UNITED STATES OF AMERICA

In honor of the Reverend George H. Fischer and his beloved wife, Harriet: Our pastor, mentor, guide, chaplain, and friend; both *Av* and *Aim* (Hebrew for "Father" and "Mother"), Papa and Oma. The love of God you have shared—Father, Son, and Holy Spirit—will live forever!

Contents

Introduction: Rigorous Relationships and Why They Matter

Not much stirs in the Texas hill country on a hot, steamy, sun-beaten August afternoon. The wings of cicadas and locusts do their best to rouse the air; even they grow weary and fall silent. But this wasn't August—it was April. The temperature was extremely mild, pleasant. A spring breeze blew across the hills. But all was not right with the world. The wind carried odor and gray dust, reminders of the ravaging fires that had plundered the area just days prior. Charcoal, cinders, and ash were under every footstep, signs as far as the eye could see.

Burnout. Everything was consumed. Nothing escaped the swath of the sixty-foot flames. The charcoal crunched with every step; clouds of ash billowed. The fire had devoured everything in its path, including the little church that had survived for more than a hundred years. No amount of resilience could keep the giant conflagration from its obsession.

L. Gregory and Susan Jones express concerns about today's pastors, and posit that there is a shortage of effective pastors and a downward spiraling into pastoral mediocrity, that some pastors doubt they are really making a difference, and that many congregations are apprehensive about the lack of pastoral leadership and imagination.[1] Add to this distress, immediately current issues such as clergy sexual misconduct and inappropriate behavior, and the evidence of crisis soars.

Oi-li is the Hebrew term for "Woe is me! All is lost! All hope is gone!" Is hope lost in The United Methodist Church? Have we been consumed with ineffectiveness, mediocrity, and burnout? Is there another way?

Yes! There is another way! The solution is closer than one might think. The path is simple, straightforward, and at the same time more challenging than we might imagine. Change is not easy. Transformational change isn't initiated with a new program or by reading a new book. It begins within.

"The quality of your life is in direct proportion to the quality of the questions you ask yourself," asserts Kobi Yamada in his book *Ever Wonder: Ask Questions and Live into the Answers*.[2] Yamada continues, "Questions have tremendous power. If you want better answers for life, ask better questions. Become aware of your own self-talk." Some of the more poignant questions Yamada asks are:

If not now, when?

How would you introduce yourself to God?

What is your unrelenting passion?

Can you really be brave if you've only had wonderful things happen to you?

If what's in your dreams wasn't already inside you, how could you even dream it?

Are you making new mistakes or the same old ones?

You will have an opportunity throughout this reading to ponder questions. The best ones will come from within you. You are encouraged to live into the question—not so much wrestle with the answer. This is a difficult transition for most of us, but a worthwhile endeavor.

"What are our obligations to other human beings? What are our obligations to ourselves? What sort of human beings do we want to become? How can we become more caring, more involved, and more helpful? How should we live our lives?" These are questions Arthur Bochner and Carol Ellis ask, which are at the heart of a type of research they use called "ethnography."[3] In ethnography, each story counts. Story helps us reach across boundary lines and pay attention to those things that are most important to each of us. Instead of arguing about who is right or who is wrong, ethnography finds value in simply what *is* and what is shared. Ethnography opens an opportunity for and a guide to ethical conversations. Bochner encourages us to wrestle with hard and ethical questions such as, *What do we do, now that we know this information about behaviors?* and, *How does knowing this story impact my behavior in the world and my community?*[4]

When we share our stories with one another, meaningful conversation can emerge. Stop and think about times past. Consider the front porch and the conversations that have taken place in rocking chairs; children playing across backyards without privacy fences; tall glasses of iced tea and lemonade shared around the picnic table or barbecue pit. The primary tool of merging thought and theory in the following work is conversational story. For those who are professional preachers, it may feel a lot like reading a book of sermon illustrations. If that is how you choose to read it, please receive this as your invitation. But be aware—stories work on us. Margaret Wheatley asserts that engagement in meaningful conversation dramatically changes relationships.[5] When relationships are strong, people trust one another; they are also willing to invest in one another. When trust is present, there is a decrease in the level of anxiety, rebellion, and demands to be met. In addition, a way is opened that leads to forgiveness and cooperation. Chaos becomes an opportunity for creativity.

Stories are the medium chosen to convey the message of this work. Oftentimes, they are personal stories. Almost all are original. You might enjoy reading with a piece of paper by your book. Write down remembrances of your own story. What illustration from your life and ministry would you use to convey the message that is suggested herein?

Wheatley also calls us to a higher level of functioning.[6] She asserts that leaders need to better learn how to "facilitate process" and "become savvy about how to foster relationships, how to nurture growth and development." She also advocates that we all "become better at listening, conversing, respecting one another's uniqueness, because these are essential for strong relationships."[7] Perhaps through these pages we can "sit a spell" and join together in some friendly conversation under the old oak tree with its luxurious display of rich greenery and wide, accessible branches.

Relationships are the primary focus of the content—our relationships to God; relationships of accountability and trust; relationships to others and the world around us. How do our relationships with those who are closest to us enrich our ministry and our lives?

What is our relationship to trials and testing? How does our relationship with our ministry and Christian service influence the "other" parts of our lives? What is our relationship with the Source of All Life?

Through the pages that follow we are each invited to practice rigorous self-reflection and examination; to engage in community that both encourages and holds accountable; to risk being transplanted by streams of living water; and to step into the charcoal and ash trusting in God, who can make all things new.

Chapter 1

In the Beginning GOD: Relationships with God and God's People

In the beginning God created the heavens and the earth.

—*Genesis 1:1 RSV*

Story Mediates Relationship

It did not seem out of the ordinary for us to have a group of four pastors standing at our dining room table after the meeting of General Conference in 2008. They were all from the Democratic Republic of the Congo in Africa (DRC). Important life-events happen around the table. Prayer. Family meetings. Conversation. Breaking bread. Sharing in hospitality. Relationships are founded and grounded around table community. It just seemed normal to have them with us.

Our guests did not speak much English. I spoke no French or Congolese dialect. Somehow we managed. When I offered to take out my photo album of my trip to the DRC, they eagerly responded.

One or two turns of the pages later, one of the pastors exclaimed, "That's John!" "What?" said another.

They rapidly began speaking to one another in a language foreign to my table. Suddenly they were glued to every detail of every photo. They recognized pastors—not just John, but one after another after another. Several pages in, I turned the page and said, "Oh! Look! Here's MAMMA Pastor!" (*Mamma* is a word used for a female leader—it is a sign of respect.) The DS at the table—*a female*

1

DS—was utterly astonished. *"That's me!"* she squealed in delight. "That's ME!"

Indeed it was. Her hair was different. She was impeccably dressed in an American suit instead of her native attire. But there was no mistaking it. The next page held a photo of her with her throng of children. With great pleasure I removed it from the page and handed it to her as a gift. The touch of her long, graceful fingers on the children's faces told me of her homesickness and that this photo was a rare item in her culture.

We turned the next page, and the next. Standing at my table were not one, but four United Methodist pastors from across the globe, three of whom I had pictures of in my photo album. Suddenly a sleepy afternoon was electric with possibility and friendship.

Ministry is about relationship. Whether it is from across the world, across the dining room table, or across the Communion table, ministry *is* relationship. All relationships require work of one degree or another. Some relationships require more work than we are willing or able to invest. They sap our energy. Other relationships are rich and deep. They take us to the thin places of God.

The gift of story mediates our relationships. One of the DISCIPLE Bible Study classes I taught laughed at me religiously for so often using the questions, "What does this passage tell us about God?" "What does this passage tell us about human beings?" and, "What does this passage tell us about the relationship between God and human beings?" Stories stand in the gap between theory and real life. Narrative conveys relationships.

Time and again, church people are willing to forgive a poorly crafted and even awful sermon or worship experience if the pastor is simply willing to be in relationship with them. It is the relationship that mediates the preaching experience. Congregational participants are willing to allow a strong relationship with their pastor to blot out and cover over all kinds of preaching and worship transgressions. We thank God for this, especially on Saturday nights.

Our call—to Christianity, to baptism, to ordination, to preach—begins with God's relationship with us, and our relationship with God. Through the grace of Jesus Christ, through the power of the Holy Spirit, God extends to us a hand of relationship. We respond. The remainder of life is lived out receiving God's offer, responding to that offer, and through our response offering that same basis of relationship with others. God's relationship with us really is that simple.

Relationships Are Not Easy

The voice of the late Reverend Dick Murray still rings in my ears.[1] Murray used to say that he regretted that the editors of the New Revised Standard Version (NRSV) of the Bible didn't translate Genesis 1:1 precisely—they added the word *when*: "In the beginning *when* God created the heavens and the earth." Murray thought the *when* should have been left out so that it was crystal clear: "In the beginning GOD . . ." There was nothing more important. Everything, absolutely everything, begins with God, and God begins all things.

Relationships are not easy. Anyone who has been in a covenantal relationship for more than five minutes knows this. Whether it is a covenantal relationship with God, with the church, with a spouse, or in a parental relationship with a child, we often start out excited, but then reality sets in. If it is a long-term relationship, our patience will be tested and our ability to be tenacious in commitment may be stretched to the limit.

Long ago I worked with a nurse anesthetist who loved to tell the story of her son. We'll call him "Billy." My friend was a single mom who worked long, long hours in the operating room. Billy was used to being a latchkey child who came home from school, turned on the television, and immediately transformed into a couch potato.

One afternoon when he was about ten, Billy decided that he wanted some marshmallow Rice Krispie treats. So he went into the kitchen and got out all the necessary ingredients: the measuring cups and bowls, box of cereal, and butter. Then he took out the jar of marshmallow cream and put it in the microwave. Only instead of putting it in for ten seconds, he put it in for ten *minutes*.

When the timer went off, he opened the microwave and out rolled the marshmallow. It went down the front of the cabinet, seeping into the silverware drawer, which was open just enough for the marshmallow to drool inside the drawer and all over the

3

flatware. Then it continued on its molten journey down the front of the cabinets, sneaking onto the pots and pans below, and made a nice, large, gooey puddle on the floor.

Billy did what most ten-year-old boys would do. He promptly slammed the microwave door and went back to watching television.

My friend got home late that night. She had had a tedious, grueling day in the surgery suite. She needed a winch to get out of the car. As she walked in the back door—exhausted, hungry, completely spent—the first thing she saw was the marshmallow cream.

"BILLY! GET IN HERE!" she bellowed.

"Yes, Mom?" he replied in the voice of a cherub.

She raised her hands in the form of a horizontal O. (In former days it might have been said that she was preparing to wring his neck.) "WHAT HAVE YOU DONE?"

Billy never missed a beat. "Now, Mom," he said as he put his hand up in a flat "stop" signal as if he were giving a command to his best friend.

"Now, Mom—"

"BILLY!"

"Now, Mom, remember—patience is a virgin!"

How can we help loving a child like that? Don't you just immediately want to scoop him up?

Can you imagine the ways our human relationships with God have put God to the test? God has certainly endured more than the ten-minute marshmallow test. Why would God continue to be in relationship with us? Because God loves us!

Likewise, relationships may test us in ways we never imagined. So why do we stick with them? Sometimes we stick with them because we love the person with whom we are in relationship. Perhaps we have made a covenant and are simply faithful. Maybe we stick with them because there is some mutual benefit—something good to be gained, even if something else is willingly sacrificed. Perhaps we stick with them because we know that there is more to life than just "my" little corner of the world.

These may also be the reasons we stick with ministry. Even when it is tough, even when it costs more than we ever imagined, ordination (in most cases) is a life-consuming, full-time, 24/7/365 commitment. It is not a coat we are at liberty to put on and take off if the time is convenient or inconvenient. Even when we are tested, we stay with it, because we believe in a higher commitment, a higher calling than our little corner of the world or piece of the story. Whether we work within the bounds of an organized religion or not, whether we are ordained or not, ministry is hard work. The excessive demands of vocational ministry require the ability to reach deep inside to build a relationship with ourselves that is founded in a relationship with God.

Relationship with Self

Many of us have turbulent teenage years. Mine were no exception—except they were mine, and I thought I was surely the only teenager to ever have experienced such chaos. I was not a bad girl, really. I just intentionally made bad choices. There was no peace to be found anywhere within me.

When my mother was angriest with me, she would say that she wished for me to have a daughter who was just like me. I lived into my late twenties fearing that it would be so. I entered my thirties knowing without a doubt that my mother's wish had come true.

Both of our children were intentionally given names that mean "God's gift." I never imagined what a great gift they would each be to us, and the opportunity for healing that parenting such great children could be. The greatest gift that our children have given to me is that their very presence has forced me to look at life and God in a bigger way. For example, the parable of the prodigal son will never be the same as it was before we had a headstrong child. My understanding of God's grace can never return to the naïveté it reflected prior to my reprimanding one of our children too severely, going back to apologize, and having him say, "It's OK, Mom. I love you. I forgive you."

Maybe it is in that context that I now read the eleventh chapter of Isaiah. You know the passage—the one about God's promise that a messiah will come to establish peace on earth. There will be a new order—predator and prey will live in harmony. A little child—a vulnerable, innocent, nonviolent child—will lead us.

When you think about it, that's a pretty unrealistic picture. Not only that, it is also unnatural. It is deviant for a wolf and a lamb to lie down together. The relationship between the University of Texas at Austin and Texas A&M makes for a good illustration when it comes to talking about unnatural peace. (If nothing else, I'll commit it to writing, since the future of our school rivalry is presently in danger.)

Ken Bassford and I managed to have a child who is an anomaly. Headstrong like her mother, she decided at an early age—around six—that she was NOT going to be a UT fan. She was going to be, of all things, an Aggie! We hung our heads. An Aggie she has been. How could I have birthed and reared an Aggie child? It's almost unbearable!

Several years ago, before the great Texas versus Texas A&M football game, our daughter announced to me that she was switching sides—she would be rooting for UT in the game. I told her she couldn't do that. It isn't natural; it's just not done. One doesn't switch college teams like that! No matter how far down the chips may be, you just don't switch teams.

It's about as "natural" for a lamb and a lion to lie down together as it is for an Aggie and a Longhorn or a Sooner and a Red Raider to root for each other. It just isn't done! But Isaiah says it *will* be so. In the Peaceable Kingdom the unnatural will become natural. It is not normal for different categories of folk to trust one another— but it will be so.

Peace? A time when the wolf and the lamb will live together, the leopard and the kid goat will lie down together, the calf and the lion and the fatling together? My guts cry out, "Get real, Isaiah! I work in the church! I know that peace is often just a superficial calm between storms. There are money problems and personality conflicts and leadership issues. Then there are those basic theological and ideological differences that cause wedges and chasms between us. And you expect us to be at peace?"

I feel like Jeremiah. Several times he speaks for God, saying, "They have treated the wound of my people carelessly, saying, 'Peace, peace,' when there is no peace." And we, just by virtue of being human, want to point our fingers and say, "They did it! It's their fault! Our world was getting along just fine until they messed it all up!" At least that's the story we hear in Genesis 2–3:

"I didn't do it—it's her fault!" "Well, I certainly didn't do it—it's the snake's fault! He made me!" As a result, husbands will forever whine things such as "But I didn't *hear* you say that." And wives will eternally snap, "I *told* you so."

Then look at this: in Matthew 10:34 Jesus tells the disciples:

> "Do not think that I have come to bring peace to the earth; I have not come to bring peace, but a sword. For I have come to set a man against his father, and a daughter against her mother, and a daughter-in-law against her mother-in-law; and one's foes will be members of one's own household."

There you have it. Biblical proof of our division. *Division.* There are many divisions. Jesus tells us that he has come not to bring peace but division. It is normal to be divided. I have a right to my grudge. I am justified for not wanting to associate with the likes of "them."

But then in Romans 12 and in Ephesians 4 we hear that we are "one body in Christ" (Rom. 12:5), that there is "one body and one Spirit, just as [we] were called to the one hope of [our] calling, one Lord, one faith, one baptism, one God and Father of all, who is above all and through all and in all" (Eph. 4:4-6).

Are we divided or are we united? Do we have peace or a sword? Which is it?

An answer erupts from my time of quiet: "Both!"

That passage in Matthew 10 goes on to say, "Those who find their life will lose it, and those who lose their life for my sake will find it." There is something bigger at work than our personal desires, something greater than *what I want.*

It took three decades for me to realize that if I wanted to have peace in my soul, then I needed to find God there too. It was only when God was at the top of my priority list that everything else had the potential to fall into place. This decision often requires a division with the world. Sometimes, it can require a district super-intendent (DS) to make decisions that alienate friends.

Before the bishop and cabinet of the Central Texas Annual Conference make appointments, we remind ourselves that our appointment priorities are to be based on what we perceive through prayer and discernment: "God, and the kingdom of God; the mission field; the church; and the pastor—*in that order.*" Do we make mistakes? Yes, we do. At the same time, I believe we are working as hard as can be to truly listen to God and move forward with courage and a willingness to follow God's leading.

Self Divided

Perhaps the most significant division—perhaps the division that is most important—has little or nothing to do with divisions between us. Perhaps the most vital division is the division that takes place *within* each and every one of us. Where am I divided within myself? Where in me does God's Spirit meet my flesh? Do I recognize that it is for *my* sin that God has been made flesh; that it's for *my* wrongdoing that Christ suffered and died?

The question that Isaiah raises in my mind is, do I have the ability, do *I* have the discernment, will I allow Christ to cause a division within my very self, that I might see where I have sinned and fallen short of the glory of God? Will I allow Christ to show me where even I have parted from the waters of my baptism? Margaret Wheatley says it this way, "It's not differences that divide us. It's our judgments about each other that do."[2]

Remember when Jesus was an infant and Mary and Joseph took him to the temple? Simeon told Mary that the inner thoughts of many would be revealed, and that a sword would pierce her own soul too.

There are things in life far more important than figuring out who is right or who is wrong. The bigger question is, what can we learn from one another? If I use my judgment against others to judge my internal self, where will I land on the continuum? Do I have the courage to look at the outcome? Remember, it's that whole log and speck thing. Examination begins with self.

Self Divided No More

Teacher and author Parker Palmer says it this way, "Our deepest calling is to grow into our own authentic selfhood, whether or not it conforms to some image of who we *ought* to be."[3] He goes on to assert that "there is no selfhood outside of relationship."[4] This deepest of callings allows us to make a critical decision, according to Palmer. The decision is to live "divided no more." He writes: *They decide no longer to act on the outside in a way that contradicts some truth about themselves that they hold deeply on the inside. They decide to* claim authentic selfhood and act it out—and their decisions ripple out to transform the society in which they live, serving the selfhood of millions of others." Palmer calls this the "Rosa Parks decision," as Parks decided to "live divided no more."[5] He asserts:

> Rosa Parks sat down because she had reached a point where it was essential to embrace her true vocation—not as someone who would reshape our society but as someone who would live out her full self in the world. She decided, "I will no longer act on the outside in a way that contradicts the truth that I hold deeply on the inside. I will no longer act as if I were less than the whole person I know myself inwardly to be."[6]

It is time to live divided no more, as individuals and as the church. There is much work to be completed for the kingdom of God. It is time to get clear about our purpose as a people, as a united body, and as individuals. There is far more at stake than our wants, our wishes, and our dreams.

One of my most important relationships is with a United Methodist missionary couple, Jerri and Bill Savuto. Jerri and Bill visited a church nearby not long ago. I make time to hear them speak every chance I get. Jerri is always full of energy and passion. This time was no different. At the end of her sermon I was compelled—my feet were moving to stand before I had time to logically reject the response—to go forward to the front of the church and offer a word to the congregation. For those who are lifelong Methodists, that might not be a surprise. For this woman raised Lutheran, it was a shock!

May I never forget what I witnessed at the end of that service of worship.

Bill is a quiet, somewhat reserved fellow. On this particular morning I observed him as the voice of God.

The congregation was coming by to greet both Jerri and Bill as they stood at the front of the church. Because I had gone forward, I was in close proximity when a young girl, who seemed to be about eight or nine, walked up to Bill. She reached out and shook his hand and thanked him for being there that day.

Bill leaned over so that he was looking eye-to-eye with her and said, "Did you feel God tugging on your heart this morning?" The little girl's eyes grew wide as she nodded her head up and down.

"Do you think it might be possible that God is calling *you* to be a missionary? Could God be calling you to give your life to serve other people?" Bill asked.

She continued to nod a great and serious nod as her eyes grew wider.

"Then," Bill continued, "it would probably be best if you listened to God."

They shook hands, embraced, and she went on across the front of the sanctuary to join her dad.

It was such a simple conversation. It took less than sixty seconds. Like the four-year-old boy who was told by a firefighter in the attack of 9/11, "Son, grow up to be a good man," I believe that little girl was forever changed. Whether she grows up to be a missionary or an accountant, I suspect she will always remember that brief relationship. Maybe because of that encounter, she will one day choose to live her life—no matter what vocation she chooses—undivided in relationship with God.

Relationship as a Means of God's Grace

John Wesley defines the means of grace as those "outward signs, words, or actions ordained of God, and appointed for this end—to be the *ordinary* channels whereby [God] might convey to [all] preventing, justifying, or sanctifying grace." Wesley goes on to name the chief means of grace as prayer, searching the Scriptures, and celebrating the sacraments.[7]

Ordinary is a critical word here. *Commonplace, everyday, routine,* and *normal* come to mind. What are the normal and everyday channels of conveying God's grace? Relationships are a means of grace—perhaps not all relationships, but certainly those grounded in Christ have that potential.

When I visited the Democratic Republic of the Congo in Africa in July 2001, I could not fathom that I was to take a word of ordinary grace to the people there. We sat visiting with our beloved United Methodist missionaries, and they told us how children are seldom welcomed in church in Congo. I reflected on the rag-clad children I had seen that day. Empty hands. Pleading eyes. Swollen bellies. All this and turned away from the church too. The thought was more than my heart could bear, and yet only an iota of what was to come.

The next morning I was thankful there were only four of us crammed into the backseat of a Ford pickup—although the tight fit kept us from bouncing so much—as we traveled to a neighboring village to dedicate one of many churches. A ceremony took place outside the church. Dirt blowing; teeth full of grit. The ribbon was finally cut and the doors flung open wide. People poured through the entrance. Our delegation led the throng and took its place up front. With gale force the side door of the church opened, and the children came bursting in like a pounding, fresh spring rain. They swirled and danced at our feet, voices lifted in excited chatter. "LET THE CHILDREN COME!" my heart sang as I looked at our team members, eyes drenched with the love of Christ welling up in that place. Let the children come!

Two days later, the children came again. This time there was no bursting forth with joy.

They stood silently, patiently, outside the "nutrition center." Bowls in hand. Eyes as deep as the well of life. Waiting. The mounds of clothes would never be enough—even though we gave each child just one article, placed over his or her tiny arms. Some were so afraid of our white skin that they cried in panic. Others were silent—staring, hoping.

There were many children who were not given clothes that day. There were children who did not receive, and who do not ever receive, the twice-a-week meal that was distributed. There were children who just stood—lingering, longing.

There were other children in the little handmade, mud-brick church next to the center. Rows and rows and rows of children. No motion. No chatter. Silently waiting.

Stooping through the doorway, I stood before the silent cherubs. My mind raced. Their tummies were bloated with emptiness. An eighteen-wheeler full of grain would only be a Band-Aid on a gaping wound.

The panic in my heart erupted. What gift did I have to offer? What could I say?

Then the answer welled up inside: *We could learn together!*

And so I taught and they learned in American Sign Language, and they taught and I learned in their native tongue, *"Yesu Christu ananipenda!" "Yesu Christu anakupenda!"*

"Jesus Christ loves me!" "Jesus Christ loves you!"

Is there a message more important, any gift more special, than the love of God that comes to us in relationship with Jesus Christ? In any language, any country, any place in heaven above or hell below, there is no greater message in all creation: Jesus Christ loves me; Jesus Christ loves you! *That* is grace!

For some of us, learning together is an ordinary means of grace. Pastor, teacher, colleague, and friend, I've heard it again and again. When we are rushed and out of time, it is our attendance to the means of grace that gets cut from the routine. If we do not take time for spiritual disciplines, we ultimately fill ourselves with empty, feel-good assurances that we can make it on our own; we have plenty of time; tomorrow will come; there is no urgency to start today.

Relationships, learning together, and a keen self-awareness—these concepts are not foreign even to those who write from a secular perspective. Margaret Wheatley advocates that we take time on a daily basis to think and reflect.[8] She recognizes that no one will give thinking time to us. We must claim it for ourselves. She asserts, "Thinking is always dangerous to the status quo. Those benefiting from the present system have no interest in new ideas. In fact, thinking is a threat to them."[9] Likewise, management expert Peter Drucker suggests that spending an hour or so in uninterrupted thought at home before the day begins can produce great rewards in productivity.[10]

Authors Linda Lantieri and Daniel Goleman write about emotional intelligence. Emotional intelligence is more than being perceptive or having the ability to discern body language. Emotional intelligence equips us to be resilient, empowers us for learning and retention, and allows us to engage our God-given inner resources in times of both calm and calamity. Emotional intelligence is fostered by routine exercises of relaxing the body and focusing the mind, creating a holistic sense of awareness of self and others.[11]

We need to spend time specifically thinking about our contribution to the whole of our work together. Ronald Heifetz and Marty

Linsky utilize the practice of "stepping up to the balcony" at multiple points in the day, including at the beginning and at the end, in order to gain a different perspective on what is happening "on the dance floor" below.[12] If these authors, who are widely read in the business world, are aware of the keen importance of the discipline of quiet time in reflection, then surely we as Christians will recognize *and practice* the daily disciplines of soul-searching, self-reflection, and reconnection with the One who created, redeems, and sustains us.

The chaos and anxiety of today bring us the gift of poignant awareness that we are in urgent times—times that are so pressing we dare not neglect the means of grace and spiritual disciplines that equip us and call us back into our grounded relationship with God, in whom all good things begin and from whom all blessings flow. It is in our relationship with God and through the discipline and practice of being in the presence of God that we are most open to a relationship with one another, and more important, with God.

Chapter 2

Relationships of Accountability, Support, Trust, and Integrity

Nathan said to David, "You are the man! Thus says the LORD, the God of Israel: I anointed you king over Israel, and I rescued you from the hand of Saul; I gave you your master's house, and your master's wives into your bosom, and gave you the house of Israel and of Judah; and if that had been too little, I would have added as much more. Why have you despised the word of the LORD, to do what is evil in his sight?"

—2 Samuel 12:7-9

Accountability

D oes anyone *enjoy* being held accountable? I don't think so. It is easy for us to fool ourselves when our intentions are good. For the longest time, I confused accountability with control and being bossed around.

As the youngest of four children, it was almost unheard of for our parents to leave me alone with a sitter. On one of the two occasions, the sitter took me head-on, trying to force me to bed when I thought we were going to be having a party instead. I remember yelling at her with all my might, as loudly as I could, "You're not the boss of me!" And then I set out to prove it. I'm not sure who won, but I'm pretty sure I did not lose.

"You're not the boss of me!" I think that is how many of us feel about accountability. We are not alone. Remember the story of Jonah? God told Jonah to go one way, and he went in the opposite direction. Perhaps Jonah set out to prove that neither God nor anyone else was his boss! We all know what happened.

Something different happens when we are willing to be mutually accountable *and* supportive. At times these seem to be mutually exclusive qualities that are miraculously held in relationship by an invisible force field. To speak the truth in love requires trust, integrity, and an attitude of "We are going to stick with this—no matter what." It's the kind of stuff that covenantal relationships are made of—a refusal to leave the table, even when it is painful to remain.

Love Is More than Bling

The bank officer's desk was flawless—not a speck of dust to be seen. Everything was perfect and in order. I would have guessed she was in her mid- to late twenties, a very helpful and organized young woman. There were a few moments of awkward silence while she was doing something on her computer. I sat there twiddling my thumbs, trying to make observations of her workspace that might tell me something about her.

Right in front of me, across her calendar, was her cell phone. I nearly laughed out loud when I saw it. It was covered in rhinestones—row after row after tiny row. When she finished the task at hand, I said, "I have to tell you, I've never seen so much bling on a cell phone before in my life!"

She said, "Oh, thanks! My aunt makes these covers. Each one is tailor-made to the cell phone. These aren't just any old fake rhinestones either. They are a special kind of rhinestone. See how they sparkle?" I couldn't tell any difference, but obviously she could. Then she told me what the name of these really expensive rhinestones is. Beats me! I'd never heard of them before. Fake rhinestones?

Real rhinestones? Is that an oxymoron?

Could that be what Paul is trying to convey to us in 1 Corinthians 13? There is love—the kind of love that is sentiment, a feeling. It looks pretty and shiny on the outside. But it is superficial. It hasn't gone through the pressures of time, trial, and testing in order to become a real jewel. This blingy kind of love is about feeling. It wells up inside and is hard to control. It is pure, raw emotion. Oftentimes it controls us rather than us controlling it. This feeling makes us do crazy things, like lie to our friends when we should speak the truth in genuine love—truth that helps us each be the best we can be, rather than some imitation.

The question becomes, How will I respond? How will you respond? Accountability and support are quickly becoming a life-and-death issue—not because some "higher-up" wants to wipe out a particular kind of church, but because without accountability we may be lulled to sleep while we pretend everything is just fine. Without support, as my colleagues recently reminded me, we are being asked to build bricks without straw.

There is no retirement plan for Christianity. There isn't a time when it is okay to sit back and coast, watching others labor for the harvest. When the bridegroom shows up at midnight, we are to have our wicks trimmed and our lamps filled with oil, standing ready. In the lyrical words of Pepper Choplin, "Wake up church wake up! . . . There'll be plenty time to rest when life is done!"[1]

Support

Without a doubt, the most meaningful, supportive group in which I have ever participated is a group of nine friends, of which I am the only female. We started out as a clergy learning and growth group. We began our relationship by sharing our call stories with one another. I'm not sure we ever really pledged our faithfulness to one another—that was something that grew with time and sharing. We are now almost six years into our friendship. There's been one departure (though we still speak of and pray for him regularly); two divorces; one who has gone to the "dark side" (that would be me, as I became a DS); two heart valve replacements; and multiple family transitions, including deaths, major illnesses, marriages, coming outs, and graduations. And all of us (except the facilitator) have moved to different appointments from where we were when we first started. The glue that holds us together is part experience, part learning, part courage to hold one another accountable, part willingness to risk saying what we believe to be true, and part willingness to be vulnerable—to become angry, to cry, to be real and just who we are.

Friends share with one another, even when we are raw to the core. I was serving a very difficult appointment and had just graduated with my PhD. Two or three individuals in the church congratulated me on the accomplishment, but as a whole the congregation I was serving at the time did nothing to recognize the milestone I had reached. I poured out all my feelings to the group. That evening they had a graduation party for me.

The guys got a graham cracker cream pie, the frozen kind with the little dollops of whipped cream on top. But they forgot the candles. In a spark of brilliance they wrapped a paper towel around a knife and stuck it in the frozen pie. But they didn't have matches either! So in another moment of genius, they lit the paper towel on the electric stove.

They sang, "Happy graduation to you!" and hollered, "Surprise!" as they presented me with the pie—topped with a flaming knife—along with a tiara and a magic wand to boot! The tiara is on my desk at home, the magic wand on my desk at work. (We ate the pie, paper towel ashes and all.) They are forever reminders of both the grace and depth of relationship that accountability can usher in.

Support Is More than Magic Words

The tiara and the magic wand came with some magic words as well. I occasionally use them. The meaning of the gift does not end there.

L. Gregory Jones and Kevin Armstrong assert that friendships are at the top of the list of importance in sustaining the work of clergy and are "learned and lived as a practice of our life in Christ."[2] How we live in the midst of friendships, honor intimacies, and hold one another accountable is a holy work. "Holy friendships," state Jones and Armstrong, "have a larger purpose beyond the relationship itself: holy friendships point us toward God."[3]

My group of friends, these brothers in Christ, recently reminded me that the work of the supervisor, DS, or coach is to free people up so they can become the best they can be. This work is not done in a place from "above" in the hierarchical structure. As one of them offered, "The quotation is, 'We are *all* in a leaking boat! Bail!' not, '*You* bail!' (while I sit here)."

Working Together

If we are all in this together, then what pastors need from their DS is the willingness to work together to create a plan. If the pastor is going to work the plan, then the role of the DS is to assist in making available every conceivable resource to help the pastor be successful. Mutual accountability is then possible. Accountability and support go hand in hand.

What wise colleagues! Peter Drucker reminds us that individuals who focus their efforts downward in authority remain subordinate. Their efforts will not produce positive results and will be rendered ineffective. The question, *What can I contribute?* is the question of those who are real leaders. Perhaps any of us who have ever changed places of work or careers should heed Drucker, who writes, "The most common cause of executive failure is inability or unwillingness to change with the demands of a new position. The executive who keeps doing what he has done successfully before he moved is almost bound to fail."[4]

A shift in thinking of this nature is radical. If we are all in this together—creating plans together, working the plan, and providing resources for it—then we are also going to have to learn how to trust one another and learn how to earn that trust.

Trust

A few years ago, the clergy of our annual conference came together at a retreat and were blessed to have a popular bishop as our keynote speaker. The room was packed as he began his first address. I don't remember exactly how he put it, but he was talking about the qualifications of a district superintendent and said something like, "Well, everyone knows that the primary qualification of a district superintendent is that you have to be able to lie through your teeth!" The room howled with laughter—everyone, that is, except the DSs who were present.

I laughed. I was not a DS at the time.

Stephen Covey explores the notion of trust. He writes about "trust dividends," explaining that when there is an elevated level of trust, the dividends are "real, quantifiable, and incredibly high." High trust is like a "performance multiplier, elevating and improving every dimension of your organization and your life." He describes trust as the "leaven in bread, which lifts everything around it." Covey continues, "Trust is a function of two things:

character and *competence*. Character includes your integrity, your motive, your intent with people. Competence includes your capabilities, your skills, your results, your track record. And both are vital."[5]

"When people lie, they destroy trust. Period," says Covey. "They make it so that no one going forward can take them at their word." Covey goes on to quote Friedrich Nietzsche: "What upsets me is not that you lied to me, but that I can no longer believe you."[6]

Clergy-DS relationships can be difficult. Like many other clergy, I have said that one can never fully trust a district superintendent. DSs hold too much power. They will take what you share and use it against you. As for trusting other clergy, don't trust them too much either, because you never know when your best friend might become your DS. No wonder we have trust issues and low morale as clergy.

How do we manage this conundrum? How do we speak straight to each other if we are afraid that the other won't like us and may even seek revenge for our doing so? In a profession where friends are so few, so precious, and isolation is a genuine hazard of the work, how dare we risk losing one more relationship? Yet, how dare we *not* talk straight to each other?

Talking Straight

A beginning step is to be clear about what we say, what we mean, and how we say it. Talking straight to each other does not mean talking down. Margaret Wheatley puts it this way:

> Conversation can only take place among equals. If anyone feels superior, it destroys conversation. Words then are used to dominate, coerce, manipulate. Those who act superior can't help but treat others as objects to accomplish their causes and plans. When we see each other as equals, we stop misusing them. We are equal because we are human beings. Acknowledging you as my equal is a gesture of love.[7]

Stop and think. How many times have we served on committees or boards—including those that qualify people for ordination in The United Methodist Church—and participated in behavior that was not honest? Covey names counterfeit behaviors, such as

19

"beating around the bush, withholding information, double-talk (speaking with a 'forked tongue'), flattery, positioning, posturing, and the granddaddy of them all: 'spinning' communication in order to manipulate the thoughts, feelings or actions of others."[8] In the name of being "Christian nice" we sidestep the real issues. We allow people to spend years of their lives investing in a vocation, and all the while we mutter under our breath that we know it just should not be. We sometimes even allow bullies to manipulate the lives of our congregations because we don't want to cause a stir by confronting the situation. We must have the courage to talk straight—not to put the other down, but to honestly and openly reflect what we are observing and hearing.

Talking straight is hard; yet avoiding conflict or confrontation leads to even greater hardships. If we talk straight, we must do so from a grounded center, lest we deceive ourselves and the truth not be found in us.

Trust Comes from a Grounded Center

A marvelous resource for understanding the way we box ourselves in with self-deception is a little book entitled *Leadership and Self-Deception* by the Arbinger Institute. It is a narrative that is best used in self-reflection to facilitate digging deep and asking hard questions. The basic premise is that when we are "in the box" of self-deception, we are blind even to the point of not being able to see our own true motivations. We need the other to be wrong, to be blameworthy, in order to feel justified in our behaviors.

When we are "in the box," it is the stuff inside us that causes us to speak from a superior position or a place of judgment rather than out of genuine concern. Our behavior is a lie, we are "in the box," when we blame others, "because when [we're] blaming them, [we're] not doing it because they need to improve, [we're] blaming them because their shortcomings justify [*our*] failure to improve," says Arbinger.[9] Conversely, when we are "out of the box," we are able to look at our self-deception and reflect on our behavior. We stop focusing on what others are doing wrong and instead focus on what we can do right to help the situation.

Focusing on what we can do right to help the situation builds trust and collegiality. It shows we genuinely care. I recently had an encounter that made me realize how powerful focusing on what we can do to help the situation can be.

20

We have a child who went through the public school system labeled "gifted" and "talented" as well as "learning disabled" because of Attention Deficit Disorder. My heart goes out to parents and children who persevere through the labels, the public school system, and the disorder.

Recently I served as one of the leaders of a camp where there was a little fellow who I suspected had similar diagnoses. Absolutely nothing the counselors did could keep him calm or still. The last night of camp I invited the children to pray and told them they could come to the altar or go into the aisles or the back corner—anywhere they wanted. They could pray in any posture they wanted. My newfound, highly wired friend came forward. He knelt down and then made his body into the shape of a tight little ball as he sat on his legs with his hands and arms over his head. I could see he was doing everything in his might to hold still. His body would not cooperate. I imagined him working as hard as he could to pray and reach out to God in the middle of a mind that would not be quiet. I prayed earnestly for him as I watched him wrestle with himself.

After an indeterminable amount of time, he stood to go back to his pew. I motioned for him to "come here." As he stepped next to me, I leaned down and whispered, "You know, life won't always be such a struggle."

He looked up at me with giant eyes and said, "Really?"

"Really," I replied. "I have a little boy at home. Well, he's not at my house, and he's not such a little boy anymore—he is a six-foot-four-inch twenty-six-year-old man. He's a good man too, a really good man. He was just like you when he was your age."

"REALLY?" he asked.

"REALLY," I said. "And I want to tell you this phase of life won't last forever. One day you will grow up and you'll be a good man too. I promise, it won't last forever."

My eyes filled with tears as he said again, "REALLY?"

"I PROMISE!" I said.

He looked up at me, and as if I might reject him he asked, "Could I just sit here next to you for the rest of the worship?"

"Of course you can," I replied. "Of course."

That child didn't miss a single word of the closing songs. He stood motionless as we prayed. We went on to a group time that was exceptionally lengthy, and he remained calm, quiet, and still for more than an hour.

I know this is an illustration of a child, not an adult colleague. But it begs the question, What could our lives as colleagues and partners in ministry be like if we found a way to support one another? What good would be accomplished for the kingdom of God!

Trust comes back to the same ability to self-reflect. We cannot control the feelings of others toward us. We cannot force others to trust us or to have confidence in us. We *can* look inside ourselves and work from a core, a grounded center, that has integrity, that is credible and competent.

Covey writes, "So keep in mind that we're not talking here about 'fixing' someone else. You can't do that. But you can give to others someone who is credible and worthy of trust and behaves in ways that inspire trust. And experience shows that this kind of example over time will do more than anything else you could do to restore trust."[10] Trust comes from having a grounded center. It is not easy, but it is worth the investment. Trust is also a result of being found to be a person of integrity.

Integrity

A conversation took place between a group of large-church pastors and a DS. As a part of the dialogue, the DS asked the group to share with him some of their perceptions of and concerns for the leadership of the annual conference. No one spoke for the longest time. After an eternity of silence one courageous soul offered that she was concerned with the lack of integrity among clergy. The DS commented that *integrity* was a word that was used a lot, with a lot of divergent meanings. Integrity, the pastor offered, was when a person's words and actions were consistent with each other— they matched.

The DS pushed harder and asked for an example. The pastor thought she might be the first United Methodist clergy to ever be fired from her church when she shared that she saw a lack of integrity in how numbers were used to measure the growth (or lack of growth) of a church. At every annual conference meeting she had attended, the conference began with the conference secretary saying something like, "The *ABC* Conference has experienced its *XXth* continuous year of growth!" At the same time, the pastor knew it was absolutely not true.

The DS continued to push and asked her to say more. She went on to explain that years before, when she was a student pastor, she had encouraged her church to do a membership audit. The membership secretary carried out that audit with great precision and care. There were *seventy* people on the roll of that little church *who were dead!* They had not moved out of the community. They were not MIA. They were not simply "not attending." *They were dead.* In the cemetery. Dead. Yet when she reported the numbers to her DS, who reported them to the bishop, she received a call from the bishop, who informed her that she would *not* be taking all those people off the roll at one time. The bishop said she could take them off over a three-year period.

"But Bishop," she argued, "they are dead! They are not just missing. These folk have names on gravestones just down the street. Really! *They are dead!*"

Does this problem sound familiar? As the story has been told, time and again other pastors and DSs have shared similar stories of their own. Is it possible that those seventy dead parishioners would have made the difference between being able to say that the conference or denomination was growing, was maintaining the status quo, or was declining? Probably not. What we do know is that what we say in the little things makes a difference in the big things. How can we expect others to have integrity if we do not lead with the example of integrity?

Integrity. Do you remember the old "boiling frog" analogy? Author Robert Quinn draws a parallel noting the dramatic difference in behavior between a frog that is dropped into boiling water versus one that is put into tepid water and the water gradually heated to boiling. The former leaps out. The second experiences change so gradual that it goes unnoticed and the frog boils to death. We too are inclined to "slow death," according to Quinn. He writes that the executive frog thinks, "If I can hang on just a couple of more years, this problem will belong to someone else."[11] Quinn argues that in this scenario there is a violation of both trust and responsibility. The consequences are significant. Members of the organization pretend as if they don't know anything is going on, and all the while the frog is boiling to death.

Our Part of the Mess

Slow death may indeed seem to be less painful, but it is still death—death without integrity. It is turning "a blind eye," "the emperor with no clothes," pretending the problem does not exist and hoping it will go away on its own. Although we as individuals might experience less pain, the larger body or the greater kingdom languishes and might even "pass away" because those who knew the truth was not being spoken didn't have the courage to step up and say so.

It is imperative that we each pause and take a look at our part of the mess. What is it that we have done, or not done, that has been a contributor to this situation? Specifically, as we talk about the life of The United Methodist Church, both locally and globally, we each need to examine ourselves. If we do not take the time to do so, how will we move forward in a way that is different or refreshing or new?

It is an understatement to say that my maternal grandmother was a large woman. She was a stout, strong, fierce woman of German descent, the eldest of nine children. I remember her hair, long and gray, hanging way past her waist. She twisted it tight and put it in a rigid bun on the back of her head. She was a registered nurse, married to a poor Iowa farmer. She could bark orders better than anybody—and you had better listen or she would pinch! Granny could literally pinch hard enough to make a blood blister.

If my shoes were out of place when she came to visit, Granny would hide them and then tell me that I had better put them up next time. My grandfather died when I was very young. I don't blame him. If I had been my grandfather, I think I would have died before my time too. Granny was a harsh, hardened woman.

Granny lived with us for a while—a very long while. I remember walking the five blocks down to the grocery store with her on a hot summer afternoon. I must have been barely school age—maybe kindergarten. Granny held my hand tight—too tight—as we marched down those long blocks. Then came the BIG street—a busy street—with the grocery waiting on the other side. We had to cross that four-lane street! Cars were swooshing by. Not one would have stopped for me; I was too small. Not one would have stopped for her; she was too . . . too . . . Granny!

Granny clenched my hand. I could feel my knuckles crunching against one another. I could tell she was ready to take flight. But there were still cars coming. I looked both ways, and there were cars. Scrunching my hand, and with that big German stride, she set out, my toes barely touching as she hauled me across.

I was screaming, "Granny, they haven't stopped! GRRRRAN-NYYY!"

We got to the broken yellow stripe in the middle of the road, and I remember her yelling at me, "Be still, child!"

"Be still?" I cried. "They're gonna kill us!"

Like a big, boiling cauldron she hissed, "Stop! You are standing on the yellow stripe. If they hit us, it's *their* fault! At least we can collect the insurance!"

I was a little girl, but I could still think, *What good is it going to do to collect the insurance? We'll be dead!*

Is there merit in blaming others if we are dead? A part of our Sunday liturgy when I was a child was from 1 John 1:8-9: "If we say that we have no sin, we deceive ourselves, and the truth is not in us. If we confess our sins, [God] who is faithful and just will forgive us our sins and cleanse us from all unrighteousness." We would then spend time in silence and self-reflection of where we might have sinned against others or where we had failed and needed to make amends. I think the idea was that we would actually go out and *do* something about what we discovered in those few minutes of silence.

Author and teacher in the Kennedy Harvard School of Executive Leadership Dean Williams offers the following advice regarding self-reflection.

> You are used to looking at *other* people. Yes, that is important, but you must now look at yourself and how you interact *with* other people to help them solve their problems. Your knowledge of your-self will come from what you see reflected back in the eyes, atti-tudes, and actions of others. But be careful, as that reflection is often distorted. To ensure that you are not deceived, turn one eye so

that it gazes inward—so that you can observe how your deepest instincts and desires drive the choices you make with and for your people as they wrestle with their problematic realities. This will be hard, even painful—as painful as plucking out your own eye—but it is necessary if you are to succeed as a leader.[12]

What difference does it make if we figure out who to blame for the situation in which the people called Methodists find themselves today? None at all. We can't change the past, but we can learn from it and move forward with renewed commitment. It won't be easy. But since when has anything worth doing or having been easy? Easy is not the point. The point is building new and transformed relationships of accountability, support, trust, and integrity within the body of Christ we call the church, so that we can stay on task of making disciples for Jesus Christ for the transformation of the world.

Chapter 3

Relationships with Those around Us

"With what shall I come before the LORD,
and bow myself before God on high?
Shall I come before him with burnt offerings,
with calves a year old?
Will the LORD be pleased with thousands of rams,
with ten thousands of rivers of oil?
Shall I give my firstborn for my transgression,
the fruit of my body for the sin of my soul?"
He has told you, O mortal, what is good;
and what does the LORD require of you
but to do justice, and to love kindness,
and to walk humbly with your God?

—Micah 6:6-8

How Are We to Hear?

Have you ever begged God to hear your supplications? At least once in every appointment I've found myself lying prostrate before the altar wondering what on earth I was doing attempting to serve God through that particular congregation. Who was I trying to kid, thinking that I could be a pastor? Oftentimes I've begged God for a word—just one little word. The method wouldn't be so important. A paper airplane would do just fine. Handwriting on the wall—excellent! How about wet or dry fleece, or parted waters? God has given us a whole book. Sometimes we don't have ears to hear.

The song in my soul could not be contained at the offer of our first appointment. At last! I was going to get to be a shepherd of a

27

flock—a little flock, but still a flock. And we would be moving back to the country as well. I thought I had died and gone to heaven. Well, not really—not even heaven offers the fringe benefits of raising livestock.

I was in the Future Farmers of America during high school, and I couldn't wait for my own children to have the opportunity to work with country critters. There was just one small problem I failed to think through: I was a pastor. We lived in a parsonage. There was not a barn out back. I was wise enough to realize the trustees might not be too thrilled with an animal pen in the yard. Yet, because I am the tenacious sort, I decreased the size of my dreams from showing calves to showing lambs and set to work. It was, after all, better than chickens, right?

During the first couple of years that our children showed lambs, we worked out a deal with the chair of my Staff Parish Relations Committee (SPRC). We built a barn and sheep pen on her property and moved in our sheep stuff and started showing lambs.

In our second year, one of the children had a particularly stubborn ewe lamb. She would not lead; she would not run; she would not be driven. If we wanted her to do it, no matter what "it" was, she would not! When we tried to lead her with a halter, she would simply lie down. We tried dragging, pushing, pleading, and coaxing. We put her on a horse walker. The dragging of her rear end around the ring left a billowing cloud of dust. We even tried a Hot-Shot®. (If you don't know what that is, it's probably for the best that I don't tell you.)

We were two weeks away from show time. Our children would have to take their lambs into the show ring and lead them around with no halter and with a noisy crowd in the stands. I was frustrated. It was about 9:30 at night. It had been a long day and an even longer evening with supper and homework, and once again, there we were with a mulish ewe that wouldn't lead.

The specifics are a little difficult to recall. I do remember the rage I felt inside. It was during the same season when I had eight funerals between Thanksgiving and New Year's, plus papers, finals, and an interterm class. Absolute frustration. Back against the wall. All I could think was, *We've spent all this money and time, and what do we have to show for it? A stupid, stubborn, senseless, slobbering sot of a lamb who refuses to lead!* Furious anger!

The woman who had mentored us in showing sheep assured me that lambs hate to be on their backs. If we flipped the ewe onto her back and disciplined her, she would shape up. I was desperate. I would try anything! Without premeditation I took that ewe lamb by the wool of her belly and flipped her over onto her back. There she was with her little sheep hooves sticking straight up in the air—all four of them. I hurled my leg over her so that I was straddling her midsection. All of a sudden I wasn't sure what in the world I was supposed to do next.

Are sheep penitent? I'm not sure if I expected her to be fully repentant or remorseful or what. What I do know is that she was not apologetic. She just lay there with a blank, sheepish look on her face.

A screech erupted from my guts. Then I screamed louder. She just looked up and blinked, giving no response other than a dumb sheep look. My frustration grew.

The next thing I knew I found myself blaring at this lamb. And then I reached down and started to slap her across the nose, calling her names—ear-piercing curses—and slapping her face from one side to the other. Slobber was slinging. My hand was wet; my shirt was wet. My voice was getting hoarse. My children were huddled in the corner of the pen observing full well that their mother had turned into a raving maniac.

Then my children started to giggle just a little, and something made me stop. There was something over my shoulder. I turned and looked. I have no idea to this day how long she had been there, but there stood my SPRC chair with her arms crossed.

Some shepherd of the sheep I was!

Running on Residual

Please do not miss the point: I totally and completely blew it! It wasn't the first time, nor will it be the last. Let me say that another way. It wasn't the first or last time I blew it. It was, however, the first and last time I ever slapped a sheep!

My sheep-slapping experience taught me a multitude of things. There was once a book in my library, the title of which was *Frogs without Legs Can't Hear*. Sheep who are slapped can't hear either. When we least expect it, others are watching us. Our behavior shows what is really in our hearts. When we say we believe one way but we behave another, the truth will eventually show. We might be able to put on a facade for a while, but it is still a fake front and it will not last. These things are true for the general boards and agencies, the Judicial Council, the SPR committees, and the boards of ordained ministry. They are true for bishops, DSs, pastors, and laity, and they cycle back around again. Sheep-slapping happens up and down as well as laterally throughout the system. Often it is a result of our anxiety. We have a show, a performance, and expectations to meet. What if we fail?

Anxiety causes us to do stupid things. Ignoring our anxiety magnifies stupid to the point of illegal, immoral, unethical, self-defeating, and beaten down. Yet many of us have instincts that tell us just the opposite. If "the people" are unhappy, then surely if we work harder they will become happy. Not!

As a result we end up running on residual with little or no reserves. One thing leads to another and we are moved in an effort to placate our anxiety, the church's anxiety, or perhaps the anxiety of our DS. We end up moving to a new place with new people and new anxieties. The cycle begins all over again.

One of the top five complaints I hear from congregations—and from pastors—is, "You guys move pastors too frequently. If you would just leave them [us] alone, we might be able to do something." Ah! How true that is! It is also true that we have selective memory just like we have selective hearing. But how are we to hear? Maybe the best way is when we simply work at it.

A DS friend and colleague told the story of making a particular appointment. A congregation had asked for a pastor to be returned, and the DS recounted how the pastor asked to be returned, each speaking of how happy they were and how well things were going. When the DS called both the SPRC chair and the pastor to let them know the pastor was being returned, both sides were aghast and told her how unhappy they were.

She said, "Well, why did you write what you did?"

The SPRC chair replied, "We figured if we told you how awful he was, you wouldn't find anybody who'd take him."

When the pastor was asked the same question, he replied, "I didn't want you to know how miserable these people are because you'd think I was just a complainer."

The DS met with the pastor and the SPRC and chided them for lying to her. She said, "Look, folks, you're going to have to find a way to love each other and do God's work together for the next year because you both lied to me and now you're stuck with it." She said they would both be very upset if she tried to move the pastor now.[1]

Do Not Be Anxious, Little Flock

Perhaps it is in the relationship between church and pastor that Jesus calls us to be like sheep—not like timid, mindless sheep, but sheep that are resilient, tenacious, dig-your-heels-in stubborn, that refuse to give up or give in. We should pay attention to that side of the spectrum of sheep behavior. And listen, because there is an unhealthy side too.

Lambs are incredibly communal. With just the least change, or if they are lonely or homesick, they quit eating. If they go off their feed, then they are too thin for showing and their muscle doesn't develop right. Then they get sick. They die. Those who rustle sheep can gather a whole herd because sheep are also exceedingly emotional animals. They place more importance on community than on life itself. If a lamb is wounded or killed in the field, the other lambs will actually gather around it to mourn. Ultimately they can be snatched up and taken away. Think about the implications. If this behavior is lived out among clergy or congregants or the whole congregation, it could mean extinction.

Do you remember what junior high communication is like? Mary likes Bob, but Mary is afraid to tell Bob and doesn't want him to think she is too direct, so Mary goes to either Sue (Mary's best friend) or Billy (Bob's best friend) and asks for "help." Mary then shares her dilemma and sends Sue on a mission—to talk with Bob.

You know the scenario. Ultimately it ends up in a mess. Triangulation has the power to cripple relationships and create chaos among friends. We experience the same in our congregations and in the larger church system. It is often our uncontrolled anxiety that leads to chaos and increased conflict. Murray Bowen posits that as one's ability to self-define decreases, anxiety increases.[2] As anxiety increases, increasingly greater attempts are made to get others to stand with us and our thinking becomes more polarized. Frustration increases, which leads to disappointment, anger, and

31

resentment. We lose the ability to think responsively and instead become reactionary.

Anxiety can infect an entire system. Bowen said it this way: "A common anxiety-driven cycle is emotional neediness in one person triggering distance in another, which triggers more neediness in the first, which triggers more distance in the other."[3] Anxiety puts pressure on people to adapt to one another in order to reduce the anxiety. Adaptation binds people together and hinders creative, individualistic thinking and perspective. As the boundaries between people blur, anxiety rises. One who is differentiated in an anxiety-riddled system will step back and view the situation from a larger perspective; he or she will become more aware of the anxiety and its influence on individuals and on the system.

As United Methodists go into General Conference in 2012, it is plausible that one of the major issues will be accountability—for churches and for pastors. If you've been watching *The Reporter* and other publications, or if you've had conversation with United Methodist clergy in the past several months, or if you are a member of a United Methodist congregation and are aware of the *Call to Action* and Vital Congregations, it is clear that keeping an eye on numbers through a reporting dashboard as a means of accountability makes us anxious—some of us more anxious, others less.[4]

Up and down the system there is anxiety that we are going to be slapped. People at every level feel it. Anxiety has the potential to move us to positive action. Too much anxiety and we can suddenly be paralyzed, without the ability to breathe.

However, we know that change produces anxiety, and so we are prone to think therefore that if *you* are anxious then *I* must be producing change. Please do not misunderstand! *If we are anxious or if there is increased anxiety within the system, it does not necessarily mean we, or our surroundings, have changed!* The cause of anxiety comes from within and all around us. The world is changing—and has been since the moment it began. What are we doing to use the existing anxiety to move us in a positive direction? Are we being transformed?

One General Conference delegate has spoken recently of the extreme anxiety and intense hopelessness that is palpable throughout the system as we prepare for General Conference 2012. Is our perception that there is no life after death, no resurrection of the body, no hope for the hopeless who live in exile or in the Diaspora? We hear because we believe! We hear because we search together for answers. Our story is not new. It has been repeated since the first chapter of Genesis.

How Are They to Hear?

The effectiveness of the changes that are being made on a personal level and throughout the United Methodist system may not be known for a long while. We didn't go into decline over the last couple of years. We are not going to get out of the mess we are in within a year or two, and not even in a couple of quadrennia. That kind of change would look like dragging a sheep around the ring.

At the age of three, a little lamb with long, dark, curly locks would crawl up on my lap for the children's time on Sunday mornings. She would often put in her two-cents' worth of ideas. Both the congregation and I loved that, especially when she was the only one there for children's time and we carried on a God-filled dialogue.

One Sunday, however, my saying, "Just a minute, it's my turn," as I attempted to get my point across, was too much for her. There were about ten children there that morning. As I went on with the children's sermon, she patted my shoulder and softly said, "Hey, hey." When I continued with my message, she moved her hand to my cheek, again patting and softly, but a little louder, saying, "Hey, hey!" I just kept on talking to the other children, until finally she could take no more. She put one sweet little hand on my right cheek and the other on my left. With all her might, she turned my face toward hers until we were nose-to-nose, and said as loud as she could, "Now you look at me, and you listen to me!" The congregation roared with laughter.

How are others to hear us if we do not hear them? Before we begin to listen, if we do not take time to self-reflect and look at our part of the mess, if we do not consider where we have erred and caused others harm, how will others be able to hear? I preached on Romans 10:14-17 at some forty-five charge conferences last year:

But how are they to call on one in whom they have not believed? And how are they to believe in one of whom they have never heard? And how are they to hear without someone to proclaim him? And how are they to proclaim him unless they are sent? As it is written, "How beautiful are the feet of those who bring good news!" But not all have obeyed the good news; for Isaiah says, "Lord, who has believed our message?" So faith comes from what is heard, and what is heard comes through the word of Christ.

I routinely ask the question of our people, "Who have you personally introduced to Jesus Christ?" This work cannot belong to "somebody else." We must name it and claim it. In addition, we must hold ourselves accountable to the numbers—not as a threat, but as a way of measuring whether we are reaching our potential. Are we doing the work we thought we were doing? Is our energy bearing fruit? Do we need to take inventory and change our tactics?

Please stop and take account. How many people have you personally brought into relationship with Christ? I know many clergy who would have to answer, "Zero." If you have not, why not? If you have, how could you stop at just one or two? How will the world hear if we do not proclaim the message? Whether the time is favorable or unfavorable, it is our appropriate response to the grace we have received!

A Matter of Perspective

Our family has been a great source of sermon illustrations throughout my years of preaching. Long before I used any of us as illustrations, we agreed that I would not do so without their permission. Our children were in fourth and second grades when we negotiated this agreement. I must say, they were pretty sharp negotiators! In addition to permission, they also convinced me that they deserved monetary compensation, which doubled if I failed to ask permission. The compensation began at $5 per sermon—until I started preaching two and then three services a Sunday and they figured out that they could make $15 per Sunday. Christmas Eve or Easter could net them as much at $20! (Can you imagine what this book will cost me?)

Things began to change, however, as our children grew older. It wasn't long after our daughter moved out of the house that she came back to join us for a Sunday morning worship service. We talked on Saturday night, and I shared with her that I would be using her for a sermon illustration the next morning. She responded by saying, "Oh good! I could use the money!" Then she paused, thought for a moment, and asked with great concern in her voice, "I still get paid, right?"

I razzed her a little about all the times she had not been around to hear me tell stories about her and how much money she had missed out on, but that our son was convinced he would be cleaning out my bank account at $15 per Sunday. Erin exclaimed, "WHAT? You pay Matthew too? I thought I was the only one who got paid! All these years, and you've been paying him too?"

Does a change in perspective constitute real change? Maybe that depends on what we do with it. Author Phyllis Tickle in her book *The Great Emergence: How Christianity Is Changing and Why* contends that the Christian Church has a rummage sale about every five hundred years or so. In the process of preparing for the rummage sale, we have to sort through the stuff that is in our attic of faith and determine which treasures need to be preserved and which ones need to be repurposed. In each of these periods, Tickle writes, "It is especially important to remember that no standing form of organized Christian faith has ever been destroyed by one of our semi-millennial eruptions. Instead, each simply has lost hegemony or pride of place to the new and not-yet-organized form that was birthing."[5]

Hegemony is a matter of perspective. It is the perspective of the dominant culture, race, or group, as if it were the *only* perspective—everyone else simply needs to get on board. Hegemony is blind to the notion that we—you and I, perhaps most especially when we are divergent—are in this together. We each have distinctive points of view. Together we can have a wide-angle outlook.

In the above illustration, our daughter had a change in perspective when she realized that she was not the only one "getting paid" for being the subject of sermon illustrations. (Just to set the record straight, please know that it was only on one or two occasions that I actually paid our children! The majority of the time it was all talk and tease.) She suddenly realized that the world was bigger than she thought. The Church could use a shift in our hegemonic perspective. The world is bigger than we may have realized fifty, twenty-five, or even ten years ago. Christianity is not the only voice clamoring for attention.

It's Not about Me

Mrs. Baird's Bakery used to be just past Koenig Lane, right across from the Highland Mall in Austin, Texas. I remember passing that bakery from the time I can first remember. You know what I'm talking about—mmm, the aroma of freshly baked bread. Can't you just smell it?

Now, to smell the bread is one thing, but when I was in the first grade, my class from Redeemer Lutheran parochial school took a field trip to that Mrs. Baird's Bakery off of Koenig Lane. I remember those huge bread machines and watching hundreds and hundreds of little globs of dough rising, and then finally . . . bread—hot, fresh, fragrant bread. They gave us each a little loaf. I remember standing in line, afraid there wasn't going to be enough to go around, fearing there wouldn't be a loaf for me. But there was. Oh, I remember that bread, passed around, each one of us standing with a little loaf. And then I remembered—wait a minute! Where was the butter? Where was the JAM? "May I have some butter?" I asked the guy with the tall white hat. He ignored me. "Butter! BUTTER!" I said, louder each time. "HEY! SIR! YOU! I NEED SOME BUTTER TO GO ON THIS BREAD!"

We live in a society that demands butter when most of the world has no bread. Jesus said, "You always have the poor with you" (Mark 14:7; John 12:8). Why did he say that?

In the fall of 1996, my youth group was invited to go to a neighboring congregation to talk about our involvement in mission work. As a brief introduction to our work in Appalachia, I talked just a bit about the Appalachia Service Project (ASP), its theology, and its philosophy of mission work for the past (then twenty-seven) years.[6]

After the youth were finished, a man walked up to me and in a pretty hostile tone said, "I'm familiar with the ASP program. And I want to ask you just one question: After twenty-seven years— *twenty-seven years*—just how much of a difference have all those workers made in the lives of the people they work for? How many people are really better off? How many live differently because you or somebody else was there doing mission work? What difference did you make—*could* you possibly have made—in the long haul of the situation?"

There was a long pause. I looked at that man for a moment— long enough for both of us to feel really uncomfortable.

Then I said, "I don't know that *I* have made a difference in any of those people's lives. But I will tell you this with everything I am, from the bottom of my heart: working for 'those' people has changed *my* life. I am a different person because of the work I do in Appalachia. Not only that, almost every teen and adult I have ever taken on a mission experience is different because of God's work in their lives while they are there. Home looks different when you get back. And for some of us, life has never been the same." This world—this life—is not about me.

Life changes when we stop and take time to get to know the poor, or when we become poor, or when we work *with*—not for— the poor. We gain a different perspective of *the other's* situation— and ours. Every time I have stepped out of my comfort zone to serve the ones who are "different" from me, especially the poor, *that* is where I meet Jesus Christ—every single time!

Richard Stearns of World Vision offers this translation of Matthew 25:35-36: "For I was hungry, while you had all you needed. I was thirsty, but you drank bottled water. I was a stranger, and you wanted me deported. I needed clothes, but you needed *more* clothes. I was sick, and you pointed out the behaviors that led to my sickness. I was in prison, and you said I was getting what I deserved."[7]

Mission: Feed My Sheep

Before we started raising lambs, I remember thinking it couldn't be too hard. A little grass, a little feed, a little water—*voila*! Like an instant cake mix, you get show sheep! Not! First of all, there is no grass or hay. It bloats the sheep's bellies and makes them look poochy. Second, you ration out feed—twice a day in just the right portions.

For three years we sweated as we ran lambs. Talk about cracking the whip! Well, it's a quirt, really. Round and round they ran in tight little circles—for sure once, often twice, a day—so that they were lean and muscular by the time we showed in February. We froze to death sometimes as we worked with the lambs, teaching them how to brace—that is, push hard against the handler's inner thigh so that the judge could feel the backstrap and loins to see how fit the lambs were.

The cardinal sin of showing lambs is to allow the lamb to become a pet rather than a show animal. Part of that is for our self-preservation. Not even lambs are as emotional as the experience of holding a child while the lamb they have worked with for months is put on the truck to be carted off to the meat market. Few things are as annoying as a lamb that is a pet, always following you, cuddled against your legs every step of the way. A lamb that is a pet won't brace. It wants to be petted, coddled, made a fuss over.

When a lamb is shown in the ring, the handler doesn't use a leash or a halter. All that is used is the handler's voice and hands. The lamb has to trust the handler. The ring is a very frightening place, with odd smells and human voices and loud noises. If the lamb won't listen and respond to the handler's leading, or doesn't trust, it is apt to jerk away and flee. People (parents mostly) hurdle fences and leap into action in order to stop a runaway lamb. In fact everything stops until the lamb stops. It is humiliating for the handler. The lamb couldn't care less—it is too anxious for its own safety.

It has always frustrated me that Jesus said to Peter, "Feed the lambs"; "Tend the sheep"; "Feed the sheep." I get the whole three-times deal. But that just seems lame.

As Margaret Wheatley says, if you don't tell the people the truth—and enough of it—then they make up their own truth. That's what I've decided to do. I think this passage is *our* passage—yours and mine. I think Jesus is talking to *us*. I'm not a biblical scholar, but I think the *Theological Dictionary of the New Testament* happens to agree with me.[8]

Feed the lambs—make sure those who are younger, smaller, and less apt have what they need.

Tend the sheep—gather strays, find the lost, and hold the community together in relationship.

Feed the sheep—this is where it gets tricky. "Combat error." It could be said, keep the sheep from eating the wrong things. Keep the boundaries of the pastures evident.

I've never heard anyone talk about showing lambs in terms of being a DS. I think there are some parallels. We talk about the DS knowing the churches and the pastors, but we don't talk about the rigorous workout that entails. We talk about fitness for ministry, but we don't really discuss fitness for being a member of a bishop's cabinet. We talk about relationship, but do we realize the profound depth of accountability, support, trust, and integrity that must be developed in order for each of us to actually do our work—with bishops, pastors, committees, congregations, and with one another?

If we are not rigorously trained, then we will not remain fit. I don't want to be like that obstinate ewe lamb that I stood over and slapped again and again, with slinging slobber and a SPRC chair watching aghast. Whereas we will need to lie in green pastures for a while—especially after particular seasons are over—we should not lie in order to get there. And while someone may fasten a belt around our waists and take us where we do not wish to go, we need to be keen enough to know that if we are being led by the One in whose voice we trust and whom we *willingly* follow, then we are not being forced or coerced.

Raising sheep is hard work. Being a pastor or serving on a cabinet is even more difficult and far more rigorous. So why should we do it at all? The only reason I can fathom is because we are the Church and that means we are *sent.*

We are called to those who are close to us—and we are called to those we don't even know. In the words of John Wesley in his sermon "On Working Out Our Own Salvation": "For, first, God works; therefore you *can* work. Secondly, God works; therefore you *must* work."[9] We are called to be the Church. We are the Church, and therefore we are sent out into the world to do justice and to love kindness; because when we walk with one another in these things, we have better insight with which to hear and to walk with God.

Chapter 4

Relationships with the Unexpected and Burnout

But Joseph said to them, "Do not be afraid! Am I in the place of God? Even though you intended to do harm to me, God intended it for good, in order to preserve a numerous people, as he is doing today. So have no fear; I myself will provide for you and your little ones." In this way he reassured them, speaking kindly to them.

—Genesis 50:19-21

Exploding Issues

It has been more than forty years since a dead whale washed up on the beach in Florence, Oregon. Paul Linnman on KATU Channel 2 of Portland reported the 1970 story.[1] It had been so long since a dead whale washed up on shore that the state highway department wasn't quite sure what to do with it. However, it became obvious by the smell that doing nothing was not an option.

The workers lined the leeward side of the whale with dynamite, unclear of precisely how much dynamite would be needed. The basic idea was that the whale would be blown to bits and out to sea, then consumed by scavenger creatures. People from miles around brought their lawn chairs and lined the beach to watch the big blast.

Linnman reported, "The blast blasted blubber beyond all believable bounds." As chunks of whale blubber big enough to flatten a car began to rain down as far as a quarter mile away, the people scattered—but not before they were bombarded with blubber. Even so, the majority of the whale carcass was still on the beach.

Every time I've shown this video, those gathered have experienced a great whale of a belly laugh. It is a wonderful illustration of our human desire to control the uncontrollable and what happens when our best plans go awry. The scene is also a good example of what happens when our attempts to manage chaos have unplanned consequences, and what happens when we don't clearly think through the consequences of our actions. Most of us who have hung around churches have experienced a few "exploding whales" along the way.

No matter how carefully we open an issue or concern, there is no way to be certain about what the end result will be. What we can do, however, is regulate our own response to the situation. We may not be in charge of the dynamite, but we can determine how close we park the car and where we place our lawn chairs!

Disruption Opens Possibility

Surely Joseph's brothers could not have imagined the end result of their scheming and Joseph's dreaming when they threw him into the pit and then sold him into slavery. Life does not always happen the way we intend or expect. The question is, what do we make of the experience? Actions others intend for harm, God can use for good. Actions that are not thought through that inflict unintended harm, God can use for good. *Whatever* happens, God can use for good.

Disruption opens new possibility. Margaret Wheatley argues that systems have the ability to utilize disorientation and chaos in a positive manner. It is disorientation that allows a system to stay "off balance so that the system can change and grow."[2] She asserts that *"disorder* can be a source of *new order."* Chaos and confusion do not need to be understood as signs that we are falling apart; instead they can be welcomed as opportunities for creativity.[3] Disequilibrium can lead to growth.

You probably know that in a small town the children go to all the Vacation Bible Schools (VBS) in the town. In fact, in a large city the children go to all the VBSs nearby. The Methodist children go to the Baptist VBS, and the Baptist children go to the Methodist VBS; and they all go to the Presbyterian VBS. You get the picture.

The Methodist church put on quite a VBS in one particular place of our ministry. The whole church was turned into a ship.

41

The sanctuary had a fifteen-foot lighthouse at the front, complete with a wonderfully landscaped seashore and pier. The Communion railing was draped in genuine shipping ropes, and there were pallets all over the floor that made it feel like a real harbor. Upstairs in one of the unused third-story Sunday school rooms was the captain's map room and study, with stars twinkling in the sky. The kitchen and family life center was the galley with huge pots and pans and kegs sitting all around. The basement was the brig, where the frightening criminals were kept locked up. (Mind you, it has been a few years since that VBS, but even the year of it I could not have told you what the biblical connection was.)

After the first night of VBS that year, I met a family I had not met before. It was a mom and three precious little stair-step girls. They were members of the Baptist church. They had visited our church a few times, and secretly I was hopeful they might come on over to the Methodist side. I stood and talked with the mom for a while until the three girls came bounding out of the church. They were all smiles, and you could tell they had had a great time at VBS.

Mom asked the girls, "Did you have a good time?"

"Yes!" they responded in chorus as they bounced around, nodding up and down.

"What did you learn?"

The girls shuffled their feet and looked puzzled. "I don't know," they each offered in turn. I began to shuffle my feet too.

"Did you learn about Jesus?" Mom asked.

The bouncing stopped, and the three little girls looked at one another. Finally one said, "No—No, we didn't talk about Jesus at all."

"You didn't?" asked Mom. "Well, what did you do?" (Remember, they are Baptists.)

"We danced!" came the reply. I was mortified.

Later that evening I learned they had danced the Virginia reel during recreation time. I silently vowed we would do better.

I made sure to find that same mom the next night. It was the same sort of scenario. The girls came bounding out of the church.

Mom asked, "Did you have a great time?"

"Yes!" came the reply.

"Did you learn about Jesus?"

Again they looked at one another. "No—No, we didn't learn about Jesus."

I wanted to crawl under a rock!

"What did you do?" exclaimed Mom.

"Well . . ." said the same little girl, "we drank beer!"

They had had ICB root beer for a snack that night.

It took until the third night when the girls were going through the same routine as before that they told their mom they had learned about Jesus.

Ministry doesn't always go the way we plan. There will be times and places when we flat-out fail. Even Jesus did not bat a thousand. It is what we do with the failure that counts.

Growing through Conflict

Generally speaking, not even church people like conflict. We want to be liked by those around us, so it is difficult to lean in to what is painful or feels conflicting and disorienting, what makes us feel vulnerable or might open us to chaos or criticism. These are not new concerns. Moses asked God, "What shall I do with this people? They are almost ready to stone me" (Exod. 17:4). Basically, that is the question of the prophets too, and perhaps it was the question of Jesus as he stepped away from the crowds and disciples to spend time alone with God.

If our pastors and our communities of faith are to grow through that place of tension, it is also where we must lean in. Ronald Heifetz and Marty Linsky remind us, "Increasing your capacity for taking the heat takes practice. Again and again, you must train yourself to be deliberate and keep your cool when the world around you is boiling. Silence is a form of action."[4]

Wrestling with conflict takes teamwork—with colleagues, staff, volunteers, family, and friends. It also consumes energy, which might consume us if we go it alone. So first, do not go it alone. Not even the experts at Harvard go it alone. They work as a team.

While one person is giving a lecture or leading dialogue, the others are literally at the back of the room listening from a different perspective, paying attention to the dialogue, prepared to step in, in a split second. At the beginning and end of each day they debrief, process, and plan for the next area of learning for the group. My perception is that their functioning is like a finely tuned and well-rehearsed group of musicians. Each one has an individual role, and they are all aware of how important they are to one another and to the performance of the music.

It is imperative that we take time away on a daily basis to think and reflect. This is our rehearsal time so that we are prepared to meet the events of the day. We need weekly time for re-creation. We need regular times off from work and commitments so that we can be revived and restored. Our fear frequently drives us to the opposite. When times get hard, we take the conflict personally. As the heat increases, so does our input. We work harder, faster, and more intensely. We think our congregations should notice that we, in great personal sacrifice, haven't taken a day off in weeks. We worked the whole week we were supposed to be on vacation. We even missed that continuing education event for which we longed. The really bad news is the conflict didn't diminish through all our sacrifice—but our energy dramatically decreased, or maybe it was drained altogether.

Creativity and Laughter as Resources

When we are beset with conflict and our energy is depleted, it is almost impossible for us to be creative. Creativity and curiosity are important tools as we move into new ways of being. They are so important that Wheatley posits that our very survival may depend on them.[5] Likewise, when congregations are ripped apart by conflict, they and the pastors who serve them lose their ability to laugh and to be creative, and take themselves far too seriously.

In one such place that I served, the first several Sundays were like standing in front of a great black hole. Every bit of energy seemed to be leeched out of the place. The former pastor was absolutely rigid, unbelievably serious, and terribly dramatic. For my first Sunday at that church, it somehow ended up that the music director introduced me to the congregation rather than the SPRC chair doing so. I think the SPRC chair had tossed my introduction to the music director just moments before worship began. As the music director stood in front of the standing-room-only crowd, she said with all the energy she could muster, "And now I would like to . . . I am so very pleased to . . . please meet our new senior pastor, Ginger Bastard!"

There was an audible gasp from the gathered body. The whole group stood absolutely motionless. The music director turned to her husband and said, "I didn't really just say what I think I said, did I?" To which he nodded and replied, "Yes, dear, you certainly did!" The congregation, who had still not released that breath, now paralyzed, waited for a response. I stepped up to the microphone and with a giant smile said, "That's OK, [music director], it's not the first time I've been called that, and I'm sure it won't be the last!" I laughed, and the congregation broke into wonderful laughter and applause. It was a great way to begin a relationship. Imagine what would have—what *could* have—happened if I had been offended. That introductory moment could have signaled the end of my ministry in that place.

Instead we had a rich relationship, and we loved to laugh together. During one administrative council meeting, I happened to notice that February 2 fell on a Sunday. The chair immediately chimed in and talked about how important Groundhog Day was in the life of that congregation—it was a BIG deal! I never caught on that she had me—bait, hook, line, and sinker. The rest of the committee quickly jumped on board. It was minutes later that I finally caught on. That was not to be the last word on the matter, however. On that Sunday, February 2, I showed clips of the movie *Groundhog Day*, had pictures of groundhogs interspersed with the PowerPoint song lyric slides, and even had a person dressed in a groundhog costume open the beginning of worship. We had fun *and* shared God!

Flush with Possibility

For a time I had the blessed opportunity to serve a tenacious little church with an average attendance of about ten in worship. The outhouse had been relocated multiple times, but as the congregation grew older, the boards rotted out, the pit filled, and they just gave it up. Every time we talked about doing something new in that little church, the issue of not having bathroom facilities came up. Then the new idea would immediately be abandoned because we didn't have a bathroom.

The way we came to broach the topic was through a quotation, I believe from Kathleen Norris, who advises that all major decisions should be made in light of a cemetery, listening to the voices of those who have gone before, resounding in our hearts. I suggested to the group that we might consider doing so. What would those who had gone before have to offer to us in this day and time? Was it time to close the doors? Would they want us to carry on? What was the next step?

As that little group huddled for worship Sunday after Sunday, a couple of them began to take on the questioning as their own, wondering what *could* we do for the kingdom of God. Almost anything that was "normal" to the life of a church required restroom facilities. The duration of our church life was an hour at best. We were held hostage by the inability to flush. The answer became clear. One of the blessed saints in that place collected a few dollars, added a pocketful of her own money, and had a bathroom installed in one of the large closets. We could flush—and wash! A couple of months later one of the neighboring congregations closed. Suddenly that little church of ten more than doubled in size!

Rising Above

Resilience is the ability to rise above adversity. From 1955 until 2001, Emmy Werner and Ruth Smith conducted a study of 698 residents born on the island of Kauai in Hawaii. Based on that longitudinal study, Werner and Smith argue that resilience is what helps people in the midst of adversity.[6] Resilience does not eliminate risk or undesirable conditions, but the quality of resilience empowers individuals to cope and address situations that are problematic. Werner and Smith noted specific traits of those who are resilient.

Resilient people tend to "meet the world on their own terms." They are autonomous and alert. People who are resilient communicate well and are able to figure out ways to help themselves. Resilient teenagers have a positive self-image. They have friends and tend to be more assertive and more independent than other teens. In addition, people who are resilient are able to draw support from others outside the family group—often ministers, youth leaders, or church groups. They believe that their lives have meaning and that they are able to influence their fate. Resilient men and women are focused on high achievement. They also utilize faith and prayer as coping mechanisms and support.[7]

The paradox of resilience is that the worst of times can also bring out one's best. A crisis can lead to transformation and growth in unforeseen directions. It can be a "wake-up call" alerting us to the importance of loved ones or jolting us to reorder life priorities. In the midst of suffering, as individuals dig deeply within themselves and reach out to others, the hardship endured opens ways for the spirit to grow. In turn, spiritual beliefs and practices strengthen the ability to withstand and transcend adversity. Such keys to resilience, such as meaning making, hope, courage, perseverance, and connectedness, are all enhanced by spirituality.[8]

D. L. Coutu argues that the qualities that foster resilience in individuals and families are imperative for organizational resilience.[9] Companies must lift up those values that are premier. These core values allow employees to think outside the box and imagine possibilities rather than be confounded. They foster the ability to discern meaning out of difficulty and to thrive rather than barely survive. Although resilience may be a trait one is born with, there is also increasing evidence that it can be learned.

Spilling over the Edge

United Methodists are blessed to have numerous churches that are resilient. The size of a congregation does not determine resilience, or vitality. A small congregation can be just as lively in faith and mission as a larger one. No matter the demographics of a congregation or its mission field, each of our congregations has the ability to be fruitful. Jesus said, "For those who want to save their life will lose it, and those who lose their life for my sake, and for the sake of the gospel, will save it" (Mark 8:35).

Mother was an Iowa farm girl. My grandfather, her father, came to the United States from Germany. He was of good farm stock—the Muller clan. I used to LOVE to hear my mother tell stories about growing up on the farm; it was rare that she told them.

Being the fourth of four children, she had grown pretty weary of farm stories by the time I came around. I think she was ready to pretend that that part of her life had never existed.

Daddy, however, was not from farm country. His father came to the United States from Norway; and in the good Norwegian tradition, he worked with wood. More specifically, he moved houses—whole houses. You have to remember these were the days before mobile homes. My grandfather used to love to move houses down narrow lanes and country roads. He loved the thrill of the challenge of moving a house from one side of town to the other.

Country met city; Germany met Norway; and the years were always rocky for my parents. My two grandmothers were madder than wet hens that my parents fell in love with each other. Actually, I'm not so sure it was my parents' relationship that they were unhappy about. I think it was being forced into a relationship with each other that made them most furious. Until the day they died they would coldly greet each other: "And Mrs. Muller, how are you today?" "Fine, Mrs. Olson. Just fine. And yourself?" But that is another story.

That German country farm girl baked bread on Monday—at least I heard that was so. One Monday my father came into the house and asked my mom if she wanted to accompany him to watch my grandfather move a house. It was a particularly wide house—and they were going across a really narrow, rickety bridge with a sharp curve immediately on the other side. My mom was all too happy to leave her apron. She quickly finished adding the yeast for the bread, stirred in some more flour, and raced out the door.

After watching them get the house through town, Mom asked Dad to take her home so she could knead down the bread. She was aghast as she entered the kitchen. Either she had had a really prolific batch of yeast, or had put in a cup instead of a tablespoon, or some other reason. The dough had risen, all right—all the way out of the bowl and onto the counter. There were huge puddles of bread dough. Mom scooped it up, put the "dirty" dough in the slop bucket, and then fashioned her loaves and set them on top of the stove to rise again. Then she headed back out the door with my dad.

The house-moving was fantastic. The whole countryside had gathered to watch and cheer as my grandfather made the final turn onto the country lane just after dark. My parents headed back home.

Be the Yeast in the Loaf

The bread had risen again. It had expanded into the burners of the stove and through the burners into the oven. It had traveled from the stovetop to the front of the stove and was now in great pools on the floor. The dough had taken on a life of its own from the depths of the slop bucket. Rolling down the counter and onto the floor, it had risen to a great height, spilling over the top and down the sides of the once-hungry bucket, which seemed to be burping dough all over the place. My Norwegian grandfather would say in a very thick accent, *"It vas te biggest mess you had ever seen!"*

Some of us can relate to that big mess. When people start acting like the yeast in the loaf, God does amazing things through us. The growth starts to look like it is just out-of-control bread dough, running out of the slop bucket onto the floor.

The overflow is where we are supposed to live! Our place with God is in the abundance of life that overflows into thanksgiving and runs down the counter into the lives of others. Sometimes that is chaotic and out of our control. Almost always, that place of abundance and overflow is messy and uncontrollable. Frequently it does not make sense. Always, if it is of God, it crosses over into mystery and miracle.

Felled and Burned

What happens when we do not live in that place of overflow and abundance? At best it may result in complacency, apathy, and flatness. More often it looks like burnout. Burnout looks like a pastor walking out of a meeting—to never come back; a church member who is active in five different committees and then suddenly bursts into tears, disappears, and won't answer church phone calls; a youth director (or a whole United Methodist denomination of them) whose tenure is eleven to fifteen months at best. Everyone is at risk of burnout to some extent, but those with specific characteristics are more inclined to burn out than others.

Christina Maslach reports that those who are inclined to burn out exhibit the following qualities:

(a) low self-esteem or self-confidence;
(b) an inability to set personal limits and recognize responsibilities;
(c) a high level of needing approval and affection, where all else is sacrificed in order to meet the personal need to achieve;
(d) lack of autonomy and control—that is, either feeling helpless, powerless, and trapped or an excessive need to control; and
(e) lack of healthy expression of emotions, such as hostility, fear, impatience, and empathy.[10]

Those most likely to burn out are not necessarily the ones doing the most work or even putting in long hours, but rather are the ones who are caught in an emotionally "responsible position for others and their problems."[11] Edwin Friedman wrote:

It is absolutely absurd to assume that energetic, passionate, responsible leaders or parents can avoid "overworking." But they can avoid *over-functioning*, by which I mean becoming responsible for the relationships or problems of others. An emotional process view of burnout holds that the stress of leaders is, above all, determined by the extent to which they become caught in the confluence of their institution's various emotional fields, not simply by the quantity of their "workload."[12]

Burnout is a significant issue in the church whether we are speaking of laity or of clergy. Burnout becomes especially problematic as congregations near the transitional sizes between family, pastoral, program, large church, and regional church models. The seasons of transition can be treacherous, particularly if either the pastor or the congregation is unwilling or unable to live into a new way of being. The congregation may increase in worship attendance, but if there is not a framework to sustain the transition, it is rare that they are able to break through to the next level of attendance and continue growing. The pastor becomes discouraged, the church participants become disheartened, and in the United Methodist system there is often a change in pastor. The congregation sees that every time there is a pastoral change there is a "roller coaster" effect in attendance, and it seems the annual conference is to blame.

Burnout Is Systemic

There is a correlation between the nature of the job and the nature of the individual who is doing the work. The incidence of burnout is higher when the work and worker are mismatched. This disparity is evident through

(a) work overload—having to do too much in too little time;
(b) lack of control—inability to make choices and/or decisions;
(c) lack of reward—need for approval, recognition both of ourselves and our work;
(d) lack of community—people do not do well in isolation;
(e) lack of fairness—we all need respect and confirmation of our self-worth; and
(f) a conflict of values—when we are asked to do work that is unethical or clashes with our personal values, pride, integrity, or self respect.

Burnout is the result of these mismatches and turns into a downward spiral. *"Energy* turns into *exhaustion, involvement* turns into *cynicism,* and *efficacy* turns into *ineffectiveness."*[13]

Burnout is not an individual problem. The typical response to a burnout is to blame the individual, change out the person in that role, and perhaps get rid of the one who is burned out. This will do little, if any, good. Christina Maslach and Michael Leiter write, "As a result of extensive study, we believe that burnout is not a problem of the people themselves, but of the *social environment* in which people work."[14]

Burnout prevention is an organizational project and a continuous process. It is enhanced when the organization and its people are connected and when people in the organization are connected to one another. Burnout is a systemic issue. Maslach states, "Just as individuals can be characterized as 'healthy' in terms of their physical and emotional well-being, so can organizations be judged as 'healthy' in terms of the social interactions among their members."[15]

"Stress and burnout," wrote Friedman, "are relational rather than quantitative, and are due primarily to getting caught in a responsible position for others and their problems."[16] According to Friedman, from the Bowen systems theory perspective if one desires to prevent burnout, it is critical to focus on the self and self-functioning—that is, to self-differentiate.

Parker Palmer offers valuable insight:

> One sign that I am violating my own nature in the name of nobility is a condition called burnout. Though usually regarded as the result of trying to give too much, burnout in my experience results from trying to give what I do not possess—the ultimate in giving too little! Burnout is a state of emptiness, to be sure, but it does not result from giving all I have: it merely reveals the nothingness from which I was trying to give in the first place.[17]

Cup Theology—Spilling Over

How does any of the above fit with Wesleyan theology? Imagine that our lives are like a Communion cup. God continuously pours grace into us. Our Wesleyan heritage would call that "prevenient grace." The problem is the cup never fills because it is riddled with holes at the bottom. No matter how rapidly God pours in the grace, the cup never fills because it runs out equally as fast.

As the grace spills out around the bottom of the cup, it forms a pool. In real life the pool might be considered good works, serving on a committee, or singing in the choir. But the pool is collected out of our brokenness, not our wholeness. We finally reach a point of being burned out, burned up, totally bereft. Out of the grace that is within us, we reach out and ask for God's help. Aha! The moment for which God has been waiting!

God reaches out to us and seals our brokenness, and we are made right with God: justification. Instantly the cup begins to fill until it is filled to overflowing. Once the cup is so full it spills over, a pool is again formed at the base of the cup. This spilling over is sanctification.

Again, it may look like mission work, or teaching a Sunday school class, or playing hand bells—but the difference is we are giving out of our fullness rather than our emptiness. Our relationship with God influences the world. We are renewed; the church is renewed; the world is renewed.

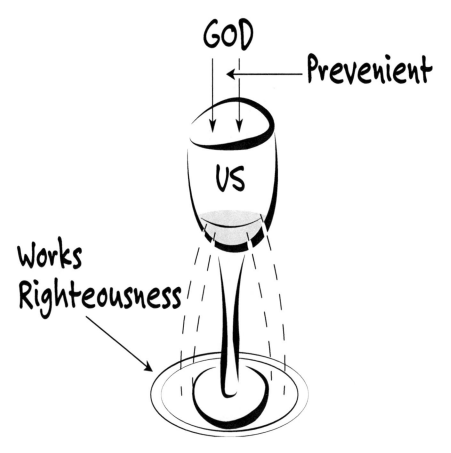

God pours grace into us, but our cup never fills because our relationship with God is broken. We may do good work in the world, but it is given out of our brokenness. We are at risk for burnout, depletion, and emptiness.

Seasons of Refreshing

Renewal begins with God. When we take time for daily prayer, devotionals, and study of the scriptures, God is there, ready to make that which is broken, whole. When we give to others in service and sacrifice, God is there, allowing us to give out of our fullness rather than our emptiness. When we take time on the balcony to be in relationship with God, we are also empowered to be in healthy relationship with one another. We see things we would not otherwise see. Instead of grumbling and bitterly complaining,

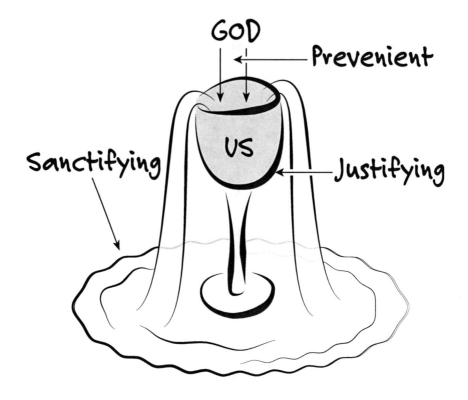

GOD

Prevenient

US

Sanctifying

Justifying

When we are in right relationship with God, our brokenness is made whole. We are able to give out of our fullness, spilling God's grace to those around us and into the world. We can never out-give God!

causing division and divisiveness, we engage in community that moves forward toward a common purpose.

The systemic issue of burnout may be fresh in my mind because I live in Texas—where we've had over one hundred days of temperatures over one hundred degrees in the past few months and raging wildfires off and on since last spring. The fires have burned hundreds of thousands of acres of land, including one of my little churches, thousands of homes, and untold numbers of outbuildings, barns, deer camps, and the like. While the East Coast is being flooded, we are in severe drought, holding on to hear the promise of rain. There are parched seasons of life.

Years ago, on a canoe trip in the Lake of the Woods area of Ontario, Canada, we discovered an area that had been burned out years before. With packs on our fronts and packs on our backs and carrying canoes overhead, it was a grueling portage. We picked our way through the wilderness of felled trees and thick brambles, trusting there really would be a lake on the other side. Every once in a while we would come upon the most unique patches of blueberries and strawberries I've ever seen. The fruit was miniature, tiny. The flavor of that fruit was WOW! We had been told to watch for the patches—they only grow in the burned-out areas. The most flavorful fruit grows in the area that has previously been completely charred. That will preach.

What about us? Are our life-cups filled to the brim and overflowing with God's most flavorful fruit?

Joseph reassured his brothers that he would not seek revenge. He lifted his head above the chaos and conflict that had been within his family for generations and realized this was an opportunity for him to begin to write the story anew. Imagine the joy at the dinner table that night as the blessings filled and spilled over their cups, the bread was broken, and the fruit was passed around the table. The abundance of grace must have been palpable. God can take the worst events in our lives and use them for good. It is in God's very nature. What human beings mess up, God can make right.

Chapter 5

Relationship to Leadership and a Future with Hope

The Israelites said to them, "If only we had died by the hand of the LORD in the land of Egypt, when we sat by the fleshpots and ate our fill of bread; for you have brought us out into the wilderness to kill this whole assembly with hunger."

—Exodus 16:3

So if you think you are standing, watch out that you do not fall. No testing has overtaken you that is not common to everyone. God is faithful, and he will not let you be tested beyond your strength, but with the testing he will also provide the way out so that you may be able to endure it. . . . So, whether you eat or drink, or whatever you do, do everything for the glory of God.

—1 Corinthians 10:12-13; 31

The Practice of Leadership

There was a great cartoon picture of Moses leading the Children of Israel through the wilderness. Moses was way out in front of the crowd. A few steps behind him was Mrs. Moses. Then way behind her were mighty numbers of the Children of Israel. Behind them was a vast cloud of dust. It was obvious that Mrs. Moses was chastising Moses at the top of her lungs. The caption was something like, "I told you so. But would you stop and ask for directions? No! Mr. I'd-Rather-Wander-in-the-Wilderness-for-Forty-Years!"

One of the great insights I've gained from Ronald Heifetz and Marty Linsky, and their team that teaches about leadership, is that leadership is an art.[1] Leadership is not a position in rank. In fact, as I've experienced it, leadership happens in moments of time, not in great spans of forty years.

Leadership is grounded in relationship, argues Margaret Wheatley.[2] She posits that the best way to prepare for a future that is unknown is to tend to the quality of our relationships with one another and to learn to know and trust one another. In his work on emotional intelligence, Daniel Goleman offers that networks of relationships sustain us when we need to get work done quickly or when we are in crisis.[3] Those who are "stars" in performance invest time in the cultivation of relationships before they need help solving a problem or are in a crunch. They are also adept in cultivating relationships of trust.

When Moses cried out to the Lord asking, "What shall I do with this people? They are almost ready to stone me" (Exod. 17:4), it may not have been an act of leadership. When Moses asked of the Lord, "Why have you treated your servant so badly? Why have I not found favor in your sight, that you lay the burden of all this people on me?" (Num. 11:11), Moses may not have been practicing leadership, although many who practice leadership may feel that way. When Moses beat the water out of the rock at Meribah, rather than just using his voice and trusting that God would provide, he was not the leader that God asked him to be (Num. 20:7-13). Did the people continue to follow? Yes. Moses led the people. But leadership was an art he practiced—we all practice—along the journey.

In the third chapter of Exodus, Moses turns aside from his sheep tending, allowing himself to be curious and to carry on a conversation with God. Curiosity, conversation, and questioning are components of leadership. In the sixth chapter, Moses takes a message of salvation to the Hebrew people, but they will not listen. Moses follows God's instructions anyway. Clarity of vision and purpose are components of leadership. Chapters six through twelve of Exodus tell of Moses' profound courage as he approaches Pharaoh again and again. Courage is an essential component of leadership. Throughout the remainder of Exodus and in Numbers, in thirst and hunger, persecution and suffering, Moses chooses again and again to intentionally live in the chaos and disequilibrium of the wilderness. He does not go it alone. He uses Aaron, Jethro, the elders, Caleb, and Joshua. He moves the people toward the Promised Land at a rate they can tolerate. They adopt acceptable practices and procedures along the way. He moves the people not only in body but also in heart, mind, and spirit.

A colleague recently shared a story with me that helps make a point. It seems a pastor in his district had many years of tenure in worship and in preaching but was lean in years of wisdom. This fellow had never planned out and led an Ash Wednesday worship service. He found himself twenty minutes before worship running around trying to figure out what to use for the forehead ashes. He finally solved the problem by making one of the worst mistakes of his career as he poured out the photocopier's toner powder into a little dish.

Can you imagine being tattooed with a sign of the cross on your forehead?

We clergy often bemoan working through committees and processes that "take so long." Heifetz and Linksy would assert that there are times when we need to step outside the boundaries of what is deemed acceptable—and there are. My observation is that it is often the times when we are working through various lay components of leadership that help us think through and recognize long-term and unintended consequences—such as the sign of the cross tattooed on one's forehead.

Staying Alive in Leadership

One critical component of staying alive in the leadership role is managing oneself. Precisely how does one manage oneself? It requires discipline and is a significant personal challenge. Without discipline, one who practices leadership can crack and collapse under the strain.[4]

Ronald A. Heifetz identified tools for leadership. The first practical tool offered by Heifetz is to step up on the balcony. Setting aside balcony time is hard—actually engaging in the practice requires rigorous rehearsal. The balcony perspective allows one to objectively observe what is happening on the dance floor below. One should not retreat to the balcony to rest. The balcony is a place utilized to strategically observe and prepare for reengagement. Those who are adept may step from dance floor to balcony and back again in a matter of seconds.[5]

One's role is not the same as oneself. This distinction must be remembered. If the mobilization of people toward the work results in conflict, and the conflict is taken personally, the whole of the work may be sabotaged. The real issue may be sidestepped as people shift their attention from the work that needs to be done to the issue of the person and embodiment of conflict. Heifetz reminds us that "The lone-warrior model of leadership is heroic suicide." Do not go it alone.[6]

We each need partners in the practice of leadership. Partners help us observe what is happening. They help us ask questions such as, "What's going on here? What's the distress about? What can be learned from the mistake? What are the options for corrective action?"

In addition to partners, we also need to learn our own way of processing information—including the ways we deceive ourselves. We have to know ourselves and be willing to have the courage to practice self-examination.[7]

Listening to our innermost self requires room to think. Heifetz says we each need "a sanctuary to restore one's sense of purpose, put issues in perspective, and regain courage and heart." It is in the sanctuary that we are able to gain clarity of the voices within and without; what we need to hear and what we need to discard.[8]

Heifetz, Grashow, and Linsky assert that *"adaptive leadership is the practice of mobilizing people to tackle tough challenges and thrive."*[9] Real leaders mobilize people to face reality and to act responsibly in order to make progress in addressing tough challenges. Again, leadership is an activity—not simply a role or a title. Furthermore, leadership is not a *mindless* activity. The art of leadership requires that we spend time outside the situation in contemplation and observation—balcony time, as Heifetz calls it.[10] Observations lead us into interpretations, which then lead us into interventions—our plans regarding what to do about that which we have observed and have interpreted.

Changing the Status Quo

Several years ago I had the privilege of participating in a pilgrimage to the Holy Land with a group from Candler School of

Theology at Emory University. Perhaps the most visual learning I had while I was there was a ladder on the second story of the Church of the Holy Sepulcher in Jerusalem. It was said that the ladder had been in that precise spot for more than 150 years because of an edict—the "edict of status quo." Because of that edict, no one would admit to having placed the ladder there— thus no one would remove it either. Five Christian groups are held in relationship in the central location of the Church of the Holy Sepulcher, but it is a Muslim family in Jerusalem that holds the key and opens and closes the church each morning and evening so that peace is maintained.

Internal change is required in order to take on a new perspective. This shift in thinking requires letting go of something that has helped us come to that precise moment in time. Heifetz and Linsky assert that in order to go through difficult change, people have to "relinquish something—a belief, a value, a behavior—that we hold dear. People can stand only so much change at any one time. You risk revolt and your own survival by trying to do too much, too soon."[11]

When the status quo begins to morph into something new, tension and anxiety increase. D. L. Coutu asserts that anxiety both inhibits learning and is also necessary for learning.[12] We have to "unlearn" the old in order to assimilate new thoughts. Real learning happens when our desire to survive is greater than our fear of learning a new way.

Shifts in our thinking may disrupt the status quo and threaten the existence of the way things have always been. Just consider the "worship wars" between people who prefer "contemporary" and those who prefer "traditional" worship, as well as both the conflict and the revitalization those divergent perspectives have brought to our congregations. Change is hard. Heifetz and Linsky say it this way, "Some of our most deeply held values and ideas come from people we love—a relative, a favored teacher, or a mentor. To discard some part of their teaching may feel like we are diminishing the relationship."[13]

It is not OK to be satisfied with the status quo. There is no treading water in ministry. If we are not moving forward, we are backing up. The church is not the only place where these ideas are taking hold. They've been predominant in the business world for ages. Perhaps the public school setting is most akin to church.

Even in that arena, there is a cry ringing out that for the sake of our children the system must change.[14]

Balcony Time

No matter how talented an individual may be, it is human nature to resist change and to cling to the status quo. When uncertainty is recognized and embraced, we tend to be more satisfied and committed.[15] Confidence stems from the ability to solve problems creatively, rather than knowing the answers ahead of time. A critical capacity for those who practice leadership is the ability to embrace uncertainty. D. Miller writes: "Strong leadership is central to successful major change. . . . What differentiates the good leader from the bad? The latter tries to allay fears that change may be messy. . . . The good leader builds high levels of commitment and resolve. . . . The good leader is adaptable and can therefore navigate change successfully."[16]

Margaret Wheatley urges individuals to draw back from the immediacy of a situation and view it from a big picture perspective. She encourages looking at the situation from the perspective of the whole. This shift in perspective demands new skills. She writes:

> We all have to learn how to support the workings of each other, to realize that intelligence is distributed and that it is our role to nourish others with truthful, meaningful information. Fed by such information, everyone can more capably deal with issues and dilemmas that appear in their area. It is no longer the leader's tasks to deal with all problems piece by piece, in a linear and never satisfying fashion.[17]

Balcony time is imperative to art of leadership. Even if the time spent above the situation is as simple as scooting a chair back, taking a deep breath, and asking an internal question, the results can be profound. I've personally experienced a body's transformation that takes place when one person sits back and writes his or her observation, interpretation, and intervention before speaking in a group. This simple sequence of steps has the ability to influence a whole body of people in just minutes. The transformative impact of such a simple move can last a lifetime. It is not an exaggeration. Taking a few moments to analyze and plan an intervention can result in the shift of an entire body of people.

Spending daily balcony time should not be a major shift for those who are practicing Christians. Hopefully there is already a routine established to engage in prayer, the study of scripture, mediation, journaling, and reflection. Stepping up on the balcony can be part of that process by intentionally adding the contemplation of a current situation into that routine. Some questions we might consider are: How "ripe" is the issue? Where am I located in this situation? How does the issue need to be framed in order for people to hear it? How can I "hold steady" and give people time to respond? What are the factions or groups that are engaged in this issue? How do I continue to keep us moving toward the purpose or work at hand?[18]

Wheatley says:

People need a great deal from their leaders. They need information, access to one another, resources, trust, and follow-through. Leaders are necessary to foster experimentation, to help create connections across the organization, to feed the system with information from multiple sources—all while helping everyone stay clear on what we agreed we wanted to accomplish and who we wanted to be.[19]

A more succinct way to say this can be illustrated through a *Calvin and Hobbes* comic. In the first frame Calvin, the boy, speaks to Hobbes, the cat, and says, "Live for the moment! That's my motto! You never know how long you've got!"

In the second frame Calvin continues, "You could step into the road tomorrow and WHAM! You get hit by a cement truck! Then you'd be sorry that you put off the pleasures in life. That's what I say—Live for the moment!"

He then turns and asks Hobbes, "What's your motto?"

Hobbes thinks for a moment and replies, "My motto is—Ya better look down the road!"

Real leaders look down the road to help people get where they need to go.

Failure

Did you watch the Super Bowl in 2011? There was a commercial during that broadcast that we made sure to capture and show repeatedly.[20] A child dressed in a Darth Vader costume is practicing his use of "the Force." The child practices on the elliptical trainer, the washer and dryer, a doll, and then steps up to animate things like the dog. Darth Vader doesn't need to eat a peanut butter sandwich! There must be something deep within us that connects with this commercial; to date it has been viewed on YouTube almost forty million times! Even with all that practice, the child is absolutely in disbelief when his extremely expressive hands are exercised against his dad's Passat—and lo and behold, the Force *is* there and there is a response! It works!

Could it be that real failure is not succeeding in what we wanted, or in a way that we had hoped for or expected, *and then giving up?* I served in a church that was an eternity of challenge, chaos, and conflict. We also had many adult professions of faith and baptisms, new people walking hand in hand with Jesus Christ, and people who came to enjoy the study of Scripture (not to mention that in three years the debt the church had been accumulating was reduced by quadruple the amount that had been paid in the previous seven years combined). It was a bizarre mixture of "bane and blessing, pain and pleasure."[21] I spent years trying to figure out what we were doing wrong, to cause so much angst in that church, but I have spent miniscule amounts of time celebrating those things that we did right.

There is a choice to be made. Is my experience deemed "a failure" or not? There comes a point where *that choice is mine!* Whether I am materially rewarded for that time or not is largely dependent on the bishop and the cabinet. Whether I am eternally held accountable for it or not is up to God. But whether our work is "a failure" or not is a choice we each get to make for ourselves. Mistakes? Plenty! Failure? No!

One colleague has reminded me that we are able to grow when we make mistakes. If we learn from the situation, then it is not a failure. We can grow personally, spiritually, and professionally. Another colleague offered a brilliant phrase about being a pastor. She said, "In order to be a pastor you have to have the mind of a scholar, the heart of a child, and the hide of a rhinoceros!"[22] We must continue to persevere.

Adaptive Change and Challenges

Almost a decade ago I was asked to serve on a team to reconfigure the structure of our annual conference. We spent nearly eighteen months working on that project. There were those who insisted that in order to bring change we had to reconfigure the organizational chart. There was a small group who insisted that rearranging positions would do nothing to bring about the necessary change; the imperative move we saw necessary was to grow effective leadership. We made structural changes, and we learned.

Today many of our annual conferences are going through the same scenario—and so is the entire United Methodist denomination. Decades ago Michael Slaughter wrote that these changes were little more than "rearranging the deck chairs on the Titanic." Heifetz and Linsky and their team, who teach adaptive leadership, would offer that unless we learn to do what we do not know how to do—change our "people's priorities, beliefs, habits, and loyalties"[23]—we will end up back where we are[24]—aligned with results that we wish were different. We are facing an adaptive challenge.

On February 7, 2004, three very special children came into our lives. They are Cooper, Dalton, and Hayden—triplets—our great nephews. Their birth weights were 2.1, 2.2, and 2.3 pounds each when they were born—just about the size of a Beanie Baby. Life is so fragile. I've worked in a neonatal unit before. However, when children like these are a part of your family, it changes the entire family's perspective.

Every "first" is greater than magnificent when little lives are so "touch and go." The first doctor's appointment; the first Christmas; the first birthday—oh my goodness, to thank God for life on such a day! Messes never looked so good; life never seemed so sweet. As you know, even tiny babies grow up fast—very, very fast!

Cooper and Dalton are identical twins, and Hayden is fraternal. Basically that means Cooper and Dalton look alike, while Hayden is his own little guy. Hayden is also autistic. He prefers to be in his own world. Interacting with the world outside is hard for him. Let me tell you about his mom, Bobbie.

Bobbie had no idea how to be the mom of triplets, let alone of an autistic child. She is amazing. Not knowing didn't stop her. She learned. She adapted. Bobbie knows just how much to push to get Hayden to his maximum level of interaction. She knows just how to coax, how to encourage, how to interact. She knows how to love him when he has a meltdown and how to help him grow and feel safe. She meets Hayden where he is, and then she encourages him to risk stepping out of his world into ours. Because of Bobbie's patience and persistence, and her willingness to risk and try new things—constantly learning, constantly challenging—Hayden is ever so gradually making consistent progress. Hayden now reads, plays, and carries on a conversation. He loves to swim.

Bobbie is really great about finding a multitude of ways to teach the boys. She uses every means available. They have a CD that they all love. It has the song "Happy Birthday" on it. Hayden loves birthday cake. He was about four or five when Bobbie said he began to understand that when there was birthday cake you had to sing the "Happy Birthday" song before you got to eat the cake.

On Bobbie's thirtieth birthday, family and friends came from all over—there were about fifty people there—and it was time to cut the birthday cake. Hayden caught on to what was happening and he wanted to be right up front in that gathering because he wanted cake! He ended up standing right in the middle of the circle that had gathered. Then all of a sudden, in a very soft voice, he began to sing a solo: "Happy birthday to you. Happy birthday to you. Happy birthday, dear Mama. Happy birthday to you!" He didn't get all the words right. He may have missed a note. But he responded in front of fifty people! Can you imagine a better birthday gift? All that investment of reaching out to him, day after day, week after week, month after month, year after year, and Hayden finally responded! Hayden was (triplets were!) an adaptive challenge for Bobbie and the rest of the family.

Adaptive challenges are transformational. That is, adaptive change requires something within us and between us to be transformed. We already know how to do what is required for technical change. We may not have a clue how to do the work needed for adaptive change. Adaptive work is risky. It causes conflict. Our priorities and loyalties have to be reviewed and revised. What we believe and value most may be challenged and changed.

While we are going through an adaptive change, the feelings of instability may be incredibly uncomfortable and perhaps intolerable—especially if we didn't want the change in the first place. We might wish to run away and hide. Some actually do so. In the church the translation could be that we lose people either way. "Thus, leadership," says Heifetz and Linsky, "requires disturbing people—but at a rate they can absorb."[25]

"It" Is Not out There

Not long after I graduated from seminary, I began to work with congregations in conflict and then to help create mission and vision statements. After about seven years I gave it all up, not because I didn't enjoy working with various congregations—I did enjoy it— but I never really saw much transformational impact from trying to help churches pull out of what they wanted to fight about, and then organize toward a statement. Congregations without vision are not engaged by a vision *statement.* Mission *statements* are not the cure for apathy and lack of passion. Conflict may subside for a time if a church has a vision statement, but unless the church *has vision*, the vision statement will be put in a closet and conflict will rear up in new and different ways. In other words, clichés, banners, and sentences on bulletins will not solve our problem because our problem is not external. It is within us. Our problem is an adaptive issue.

Adaptive Organizations

Heifetz, Grashow, and Linsky outline five key qualities of adaptive organizations.[26] They invite the reader to pause for reflection and make observations from the balcony. You are invited to do the same.

Are you willing to name the elephant in the room? What happens in your church if someone dares to do so? Is an opinion that does not maintain the status quo tolerated in your district or annual conference? If we are The *United* Methodist Church, where do we allow disagreement? On a day-to-day basis, who is allowed to define on what basis we are united, or is that something into which we mindlessly fall?

I was a senior in seminary and taking polity. I posed a question to the professor: "I grew up Lutheran. I went to my pastor when I was a young adult and asked, 'Pastor, what does the Church believe about X?' My pastor gave me a direct answer. I pushed again. 'What if I don't believe that?' He replied, 'Well, then I guess you are not a Lutheran!' So professor, I continued, about what is it that you would say to me, were I to ask, that if I did not agree I would not be a United Methodist?"

My professor opened his mouth to speak, and then closed it. He turned to one side of the room and pointed his finger, and then turned back. He scratched his head. He pointed his finger, opened his mouth, turned to one side, and then reversed all three. Finally a voice (female, I will add) came from the back of the room and said, "The itinerant system!" The class roared with laughter. The truth was no one really knew the answer.

How do you share responsibility? Do the people in your church, your district, your annual conference work alone, in silos, or is the burden of the work shared? What about the solution to problems? Are solutions worked out in open conversation, or behind closed doors? Are answers manipulated ahead of time?

What about disagreement? Is it tolerated? Are people encouraged to think for themselves and practice independent judgment? What happens if a new idea is put into action and then fails? Does the body learn from the failure? Do people respond to failure by saying, "I told you not to try that idea! We've never done it that way before!"

Are you working to develop the next generation of leaders? Is one generation mentoring the next? If someone were to ask a member of your church, district, or annual conference what the plan is for growth, how would the member respond?

Finally, do those who practice leadership make the time and take the time for reflection? Do they engage in continuing learning together? Are they willing to hear divergent perspectives and ideas about how the work could be accomplished?

If we judge the future of The United Methodist Church by these standards, are we an adaptive organization? Maybe not yet; but we are slowly headed in that direction. Across our annual conference and across the denomination there is robust conversation taking place that recognizes we must make changes.

There are also those who will refuse to engage in the conversation. There are pastors who refuse to take part in any type of learning made available to them, who will not engage in conversation of a new way or a new day of ministry. There are congregations that insist they are doing all they can to reach out, when the best they have to offer is the offering of a monthly potluck for the membership. What are we to do with them? We cannot change other people. We can only change ourselves. If pastors or congregations refuse to learn or take the steps needed to "make disciples of Jesus Christ for the transformation of the world," then perhaps the best thing to do is let them be and focus our energies where we can make a difference.

A Future with Hope

A couple of years ago my husband Ken and I went to pick up my childhood pastor, George Fischer, and his wife, Harriet. George became my pastor when I was about nine. He is the pastor who confirmed me. When we talked about getting married, George Fisher was the only pastor I would consider. Ken felt the same because George was also his chaplain in the National Guard—the only pastor who would sit, drink a beer, and actually engage in conversation. George and Harriet are baptismal sponsors for one of our children. But more than that . . .

My dad died when I was twenty; Ken's dad died when I was twenty-six. George is the only real father figure that I have been able to hold on to all these years. What we were profoundly grieved to learn was that the medical professionals think George is in the early stages of Alzheimer's. You can see he is already beginning to fade a bit. We didn't know that at the time we planned our trip. We simply wanted to take George and Harriet to see the Garrison Keillor radio program, *Prairie Home Companion*, in Abilene because we love them so dearly and because they are the ones who introduced us to the program years ago. It was better than Christmas. We drove to Lometa, picked them up, and then had a delightful weekend providing the very best for two people who have shown us God and who have been mediators of Christ to both of us.

Keillor was spot-on that Saturday night. The show was absolutely stellar. It was tailor-made for a Lutheran and a Methodist preacher—the performers sang hymn after hymn, and

Keillor picked on the Church of Christ and the Baptists in a wonderful way, while he left the Lutherans and the Methodists alone! The show began with the singing of the national anthem and ended with the Doxology. It was just out of this world.

After the show, when we were all embracing and laughing and thanking one another, George was fully himself. And he looked at me and said, "You know, we're just simple country folk, and sometimes we live such a sheltered life. Our world is so small— our little house and sixty acres in Lometa. We go to church, to the grocery store, and to the doctor, but we don't get out in the world much. And it's easy to get bitter and resentful. But what this show, this night together, has helped me see is that the world is not all bad. There IS still hope! There is still hope."

"Yeah, George, there is plenty to hope for," I replied.

Hope Will Not Let Us Go

Hope that is grounded in faith is the hope of which we hear in Romans 5:3-5, "knowing that suffering produces endurance, and endurance produces character, and character produces hope, and hope does not disappoint us, because God's love has been poured into our hearts through the Holy Spirit that has been given to us." God is still God, and we are not. Who knows how The United Methodist Church may ultimately change or not change? Who knows if we as a denomination will live or die? Is that the point of our hope? There are many of us who love The United Methodist Church. We have the best theology ever! I pray The United Methodist Church is brought to new life. I also know the institution is not the foundation of our hope.

God has been the source of our hope since before time began— not a denomination or an individual or even a group of individuals. *God alone.* Just as God led Moses and the Children of Israel, it may be God who is leading us as a denomination into a time of wilderness. This is the same God who experienced the suffering of the people in Egyptian slavery.[27] Who knows what we will encounter! Our challenge is to stay focused on God, lead when the opportunity presents itself, help our neighbors along the way, and be ready to give an accounting for the hope that is within us. Our hope is in One who knows our suffering completely—our Lord Jesus Christ!

69

Chapter 6

Relationship to the Vocation of Ministry and Full-time Christian Service

Simon Peter said to them, "I am going fishing." They said to him, "We will go with you." They went out and got into the boat, but that night they caught nothing.

Just after daybreak, Jesus stood on the beach; but the disciples did not know that it was Jesus. Jesus said to them, "Children, you have no fish, have you?" They answered him, "No." He said to them, "Cast the net to the right side of the boat, and you will find some." So they cast it, and now they were not able to haul it in because there were so many fish. That disciple whom Jesus loved said to Peter, "It is the Lord!" When Simon Peter heard that it was the Lord, he put on some clothes, for he was naked, and jumped into the sea.

—*John 21:3-7*

Go Fish!

Those who are ordained in The United Methodist Church are ordained into a lifelong vocation of connecting people to God. In order to live out that call, we too have to be caught.

Do you love to fish? Really? Do you love to fish?

My daddy is the reason I love to fish. He loved to fish—I don't *think* it was just to get away from Momma. He really loved to fish, and he shared that love with me. Next to hunting four-leaf clovers, more than anything else, my daddy loved to fish. Don't get me wrong, he liked to *catch* fish, but more than that, he loved *to* fish!

Daddy took me fishing off the dock at the Capital Rod and Gun Club out on Lake Travis in the blazing heat of Texas summer. We fished together inside the marina when it was below thirty degrees outside (remember, this is Texas, so it was not thirty degrees below). We fished in shallow water. We fished in deep, deep water. My daddy just loved to fish.

And Daddy wasn't satisfied with just fishing on Lake Travis. We went down south and fished off the Texas coast. We fished off of jetties and piers. We fished early in the morning and late into the night. I vaguely remember one trip we took deep-sea fishing. All I can really recall about that trip was that it was swell.

It was just two years after Daddy died that my husband, Ken, and I took a group of high school youth on a wilderness canoe trip to Ontario, Canada, in the Lake of the Woods. We had been on the water for eight days—that is, eight days without seeing another human being besides those in our group; eight days of paddling, fighting the biting black flies and mosquitoes; eight days of eating dehydrated food, peanut butter out of a squeeze bag, and trail mix. On the evening of the eighth day, it was time to go fish.

When Alzheimer's sets in, I want to remember that time of fishing. The sun was just beginning to bow its head in the western sky. We found a spot full of reeds and lily pads. It looked like an awful place to fish with lures. But we did it anyway.

This is no fish story. There were four of us in two canoes. As soon as a line hit the water we caught a fish. Bass. Big bass. The lake was full of big bass—three-, four-, five-, and six-pound bass— fighting bass; hungry bass. And walleye too. There was even a northern pike on somebody's line. We reeled them in so fast that I started bringing them in to the *William Tell Overture*—ta dum, ta dum, ta dum, dum dum. It was wonderful. When we had caught more fish than we knew our group of twenty could eat for a late-night supper and for breakfast the next morning, we stopped. I have the slides if you ever want to see them. Fish this—THIS— long. I caught the biggest. Really, I did!

Now, there's one thing about that time of fishing. It was the RIGHT time. It was absolutely clear as the sun began to set. We remembered that patch of reeds. It was time to go fish. The air was cool. The mosquitoes and flies were quiet for the moment. It was time.

How do we know when it's time to go fishing? Sometimes it takes the shadow of death before it begins to dawn on us that it is time. Sometimes we have to be near starvation before we realize it. Sometimes we have to be spiritually empty, void, hollow. Maybe it takes something tragic, like the loss of someone we dearly love. Or maybe it is something less drastic, like general malaise or depression. Maybe it's the bottom of a bottle or the end of a rope.

Then it begins to dawn on us: "It's time to go fishing." It's time to take a break from the overwrought business of our lives and sit and listen to the wind in the reeds and the frogs on the lily pads. It's time to be still and wait; time to collect our wits so we can then move forward in life with purpose.

Being Caught

In order to catch a good fish, we must first be caught. We first have to be convinced that we are doing what we need to be doing—otherwise fishing is the most miserable thing in the world. Time drags on for an eternity. And those mosquito and fly bites are almost unbearable. Have you ever been fishing when you just couldn't catch a thing? Sitting on a hot, Texas tank dam in ninety-eight-degree weather, sweating in the afternoon, locusts buzzing in the pasture nearby?

The line coming up empty.

That's when Jesus tells us, as he told Peter, "Put your nets into deeper water!"

Peter didn't like hearing that—and really, we don't like it much either.

I can hear Peter saying, "Lord, look, *we've tried it that way before!* And it just won't work!"

Isn't that what we tell Christ? "Look, Lord, we've tried all the church growth ideas, all the evangelism techniques, all the fancy do-it-up-right schemes. We've started new programs; we've tried doing VBS again. We've worked harder and smarter. And it just won't work!" My brothers and sisters in Christ, we need to be caught.

Just One Thing

I was in my first appointment, down in Navarro County. Our little school was having some problems. A sixth-grade boy had shot himself in the head playing Russian roulette with six other children from kindergarten through sixth grade watching. Some of them had made a suicide pact and had been involved in gang activity. After I went to a program to learn about gang intervention, I spent a day with six of the juvenile probation officers of Ellis County. They were wonderful and helped me learn so much.

Toward the end of the day, I gathered up all my courage and asked that group, who knew more troubled teens than most of our churches will ever meet, "If there was one thing you could say to our churches, what would it be?"

I promised that if I ever had an opportunity to address this great body of United Methodists, I would share with you what they said. Now, I am not going to use their exact words, but it will be close.

They said, "Tell your people to get their *backsides* out of the pew and onto the streets, because THAT is where our kids are! Gangs know that. That is where they recruit. And tell your church that IF one of our kids should happen to wander *inside* the church (but don't worry, that probably won't happen), they only get *one* chance. Don't treat them like they are weird or bad. Just love them."

Do you LOVE to fish?

There is a difference between fishing because we love to fish and fishing to boost the numbers or bring in the bucks. Friends, those are NOT the reasons we are supposed to fish! We are supposed to fish because that is what we are called to do. It is the fabric of who we are. It is the air we breathe. When we fish because we love to fish, when we love to fish so much that we are willing to put our nets into deep water or—as the language in the similar story in the Gospel of John says—when we cast our nets on the *other side* of the boat, when we fish because we *know* it is time to go fishing, well, there is just nothing as magnificent as that.

Bait on the Line

The numbers of those retiring and those coming into ministry are frightening—on that we can agree. I know the educational process of becoming a clergyperson is long and arduous. The last time I counted, I think it was a minimum of eight years from beginning to end. That is a long chunk of time—one-third of a twenty-four-year-old's life. In 1 Timothy 5:22 we read, "Do not ordain anyone hastily." This is not difficult in the United Methodist process. If we are going to have clergy in place—deacons, local pastors, *or* elders—before the great tsunami of retirements within the next ten years, then we must change. The solution is not in adding yet one more layer of lay ministry. We have plenty of youths and young adults who are willing to make the sacrifices of ministry. The form of how ministry looks is going to have to take a different shape.

It seems odd that "Betsy" was the first one who taught me about this shift. Betsy was a woman who had endured more misery in her lifetime than I could ever imagine. To say that she had had a hard life is a drastic understatement. Betsy was the survivor of a life that had battered her with one bitter assault after another. She grew up lost somewhere in the midst of the birth order of sixteen children. She watched three of her siblings die at a very early age. Her father and her husband had been coal miners, as was her son. Her son alone had been in the mines on seven different occasions during cave-ins. Betsy was well acquainted with standing at the mouth of the mine, holding her breath, trembling in fear, as they brought out the battered bodies of the injured men.

One afternoon, as we sat in the cool breeze that blew across the mountains, Betsy told me a story about a time when the cave-in was so severe that a large number of men had been injured and several had been killed. She said, "You know, them mines, they wasn't safe. Even as they was pullin' the last of the bodies out of the mine, the foreman was tellin' 'em to go back in and get to work."

"The miners didn't have no choice," Betsy said. "They went on strike. And oh, Lordy, was it a long one. The union tried to stand behind us, but soon enough the money ran out. There wasn't even enough to buy beans. And the coal company jacked up the prices so bad at the company store that none of us could afford to eat. We would go for days with nothin' to put in our bellies. Then the day finally came when my husband couldn't take it no more. He broke the picket line and went back to work. Ever'body in the whole town hated us. But that was the last stretch of his time. Not long after, he took black lung and died."

Betsy was stricken with grief at her husband's death. But maybe there was just a breath of life in that grief. You see, although his death meant the end of her means of support, it also meant the end of the beatings he used to inflict upon her when times were really lean and hard.

Shortly after, Betsy's son moved her to a small piece of land. That's where I met her. He built her a little shanty out of tarpaper and plastic. After her son tapped her into the neighbor's "borrowed" electricity, he left, and Betsy spent her days cultivating the wild poke and dandelions that grew in her yard. She subsisted on these along with an occasional wild rabbit. Just when things began to look a little brighter for her, a violent storm blew up. Lightning struck nearby, and her little shanty caught fire and burned to the ground.

So Much and So Little

I don't know about you, but for most of my life I have had so much. I've been insulated and isolated from people like Betsy. I have tried to fill my life with peace from the world, and I am here to tell you, it won't work! My relationship with Betsy was a step along the journey that called me back and moved me forward into hearing God's call.

Unlike most mountain folk, who are born and who die in the same area, Betsy was a stranger to those who lived around her. Because she was a "newcomer" to the area, Betsy was the topic of most of the community gossip. The boys in that old holler used to torment her with mean tricks and would steal the few possessions she had managed to accumulate. It seemed that the whole world was against her. Even when her son did manage to build her a new place to live—this time out of two-by-fours and tarpaper—the rats were so bad they ran her out.

That wasn't the end of her troubles. She developed skin cancer on her face. By the time she got to a doctor to have it treated, the cancer had eaten into the bone. Betsy had to have extensive surgery to remove the cancer. The surgery left the side of her face paralyzed. Her mouth drooped to one side and she constantly drooled. Her shoulder was drawn up toward the side of her face.

She had had a considerable amount of skin grafting done, so not only was the skin on the side of her face and neck disfigured, it was also discolored. After her many surgeries, Betsy was ashamed to go out in public. She stopped going to church, where she had frequently led worship and singing. Before long, friends stopped calling on her. Betsy was totally alone.

So it came to be that when I met Betsy, she lived like a hermit, in an old broken-down yellow school bus. Had I known her story, it would have been no surprise when she met us at the door of the bus with a double-barreled shotgun in one hand and a flashlight in the other.

I thought I had gone to minister to someone like Betsy. I thought I had gone there to share my gifts, my graces, and my talents. I thought the group of youth I had taken could actually bring about some wonderful change in Betsy's life, that we could in some way influence and improve her conditions. I was dead wrong.

During those few days we spent together, I noticed something about Betsy that I had never seen in anyone before. It seemed to me that life had hit her with one blow after another and yet she managed to smile, to laugh, and to joke with us all. I just couldn't figure it out.

I can still hear Betsy's soft Southern drawl as she told us, "My daddy was a fireside kind of man. Each evenin' after the dishes was done, our beds turned down, and everybody was in their nightclothes, Daddy would say, 'Now chil'ren, take your places!'" She clapped her hands in quick succession, and then continued, "We each took our special seat around the fireplace. At that time there was thirteen of us, so we each had to have our own place so we could all fit. Daddy would read to us from the Bible. Then he would take out his guitar and we would all sing. We sang the old hymns. What's that one? It starts out, 'Amazin'—Amazin' grace'?" Her voice cracked as she tried to sing the words. "Do you know it?" she asked.

"Yes," I quietly replied. "I know it."

"Sing it," she commanded. As Betsy's tired old voice blended with mine, God was palpable. "Amazing grace, how sweet the sound."

Culture of the Call

Perhaps what the phrase "culture of the call" identifies is not the need for some special program or youth rally, but instead the willingness on the part of those of us who serve in ministry to speak up when we see someone else who has the gifts of ministry. We are the ones who need to stop with our business and take the time to *do* some ministry. Perhaps it is the adult leadership—laity and clergy alike—who ought to attend "culture of the call" weekends so that we can practice having the courage to be on the level with others and vulnerably admit that we felt God moving and ask, "Did you feel God tugging at your heart too?"

What I wonder is, is our crisis really that of clergy who are bitter and burned out to the point that they fail to encourage those who are passionate and eager to give their entire lives in service to God? I wonder if we have a crisis of Christians who are mature in years of service but not in discipleship. Kenda Creasy Dean offers this challenge in a powerful way:

> Since the religious and spiritual choices of American teenagers echo, with astonishing clarity, the religious and spiritual choices of the adults who love them, lackadaisical faith is not young people's issue, but ours. Most teenagers are perfectly content with their religious worldviews; it is churches that are—rightly—concerned. So we must assume that the solution lies not in beefing up congregational youth programs or making worship more "cool" and attractive, but in modeling the kind of mature, passionate faith we say we want young people to have. [1]

About two years ago my district started talking out loud about young people who felt called to go into ordained ministry and full-time Christian service. Three brave high school youth responded at the beginning. Then we conducted the first youth lay-speaking class in our annual conference and utilized the participants for pulpit supply. Eighteen months later we had seventeen on our contact list and twelve to fifteen regularly show up at our gatherings! Increase of attendance and involvement hasn't taken a program or any special advertising or fundraisers or even T-shirts. Conversation and fellowship are generally the means by which we share together, build relationship, and receive God's grace—with a little Methodist food thrown in for good measure. For this passionate group of teenagers (high school and college) life is all about relationship—relationship with God, relationship with one another, and relationship with the world God "has created and is creating." Each of these relationships is mediated by God's grace.

Mentor in Christ

Who ordained you into ministry? is a powerful question and one worth pondering. Who ordained you into ministry? Perhaps the bishop laid her hands upon your head and ordained you to serve God through the Church, but who first ordained you to serve God? Who helped you hear and understand that God was—God is—calling you? Who helped you clarify that God was—God is—calling you to be set apart?

For Esther, it was her uncle Mordecai; for Samuel, his mother and then later Eli; for the Ethiopian Eunuch, Philip; for Peter, Cornelius. In every generation God raises up people who are courageous and bold, who are willing to follow God and encourage others to do the same. For whom are you a mentor in Christ?

How many of us pray for our children to live out their call in God? Is there anything sweeter than seeing one of our own being baptized in the waters of God's grace? What about on the other side? Do we continue to encourage our beloved to live into the fullness of who God has called her or him to be in the world?

When that same child announces that he is going to give the rest of his life serving as a missionary teaching farming to the people of Africa, when she proclaims that in order to follow God she will serve a gang-infested inner city and work with the children there, when he quietly says, "Mom, Dad, this is what I am called to do," and you know that decision may cost him his life and at the very least will evoke times of bitter suffering, how do we respond in *those* times? Did we once have those "I can change the world!" dreams only to watch them fade with the graying of the years?

In whom have you observed God at work? Whom have you noticed that God might be calling to be set apart? What have you done about that observation? Are you intentionally mentoring that person? Have you had coffee or at least a brief conversation? Are you helping others see that God may be calling them into full-time ordination or Christian service?

A New Day in Ministry

This day is a new day in ministry for many of us. Maintaining the status quo is no longer good enough. Reading a *Barclay's Commentary* and preaching based on what is found there won't make the grade. I've heard it said repeatedly, "There just isn't a call for 'nice' pastors anymore." The Church—The United Methodist Church—needs people who can exercise the art of leadership, who have great vision and dream big dreams, and who have courage and are willing to risk in profound ways.

We are not alone in this arena. Educator, administrator, and teacher of teachers Tony Wagner would relate to our situation. He reflected on his first administrative role saying, "I had a *real* problem. It quickly became clear to me that virtually all the teachers in this school felt that the school in general, and their teaching in particular, was just fine the way it was. More than fine, in fact—they thought it was truly wonderful!"[2]

Later he says of the teaching profession, "As a profession, we are extremely reluctant to criticize or evaluate one another." He continues, "The reality is that, even if administrators wanted to evaluate their teachers more effectively, they have not been trained to assess teaching or to coach teachers."[3] Get a group of bishops or DSs together; it won't be five minutes until you hear this kind of conversation almost verbatim. There's more. Wagner offers, "We know that isolation is the enemy of improvement in education—and in all other professions."[4] This statement is profoundly true in ministry. We are learning in many times and places that sharing and collaboration are key to surviving and thriving in ministry.

There is another major consideration. We live within a system that is not a call system—it is an itinerant system. In the best moments, the itinerant system and appointive processes are about the dissemination of effective leadership. In the course of making appointments a pastor who very well may deserve a particular move may not be available at the specific time the move is open. Five years later, when the pastor looks back, he or she may think, *I should be at that church. I deserved that move.* She or he very well may have. But in the process the pastor may forget (or may never have known) that the church was in the middle of a building program, a capital campaign, or a challenge that precluded the pastor from being considered for that move at the time and perhaps for other moves as well. The point is this: the appointive process is designed to help our churches be *effective and fruitful* for the kingdom of God.

Show Us the Way

Church after church asks the question, "But pastor, what are we supposed *to do* in order to grow?" Then they expect the new pastor to offer the "right" answer. Listen to what Ronald Heifetz and Marty Linsky have to offer us:

> When people look to authorities for easy answers to adaptive challenges, they end up with dysfunction. They expect the person in charge to know what to do, and under the weight of that responsibility, those in authority frequently end up faking it or disappointing people, or they get spit out of the system in the belief that a new "leader" will solve the problem. In fact, there's a proportionate relationship between risk and adaptive change: The deeper the change and the greater the amount of new learning required, the more resistance there will be and, thus, the greater the danger to those who lead.[5]

It sounds as if Heifetz and Linsky have been in on some of our cabinet meetings or have visited our annual conferences.

Margaret Wheatley asserted that organizational intelligence is a systemwide capacity to interpret what is going on within the organization. Organizational intelligence is directly linked to how well information is disseminated and the openness and communication of its leadership. She posited, "Everybody needs information to do their work. We are so needy of this resource that if we can't get the real thing, we make it up."[6] That's how rumors get started and gossip is spread. She says that people know information "is critical to their ability to do good work. They know when they are starving." Wheatley argued that the way to facilitate organizational intelligence and quash rumors is to share ample accurate information and to take a step back and focus on the processes that are at work.

Annual conference leadership would do well to heed Wheatley's assertions. Dissemination of accurate information regarding the appointive process and disclosure of criteria used in making appointments could benefit both elders and local churches. Local churches and pastors must be honest and open with conference leadership as well.

The Banner of the Lord

Do you recall the story of Israel fighting the people of Amalek at Rephidim, found in Exodus, chapter 17? Moses held his staff up with both hands. As long as the people of Israel, who were fighting in the valley below, could see the banner, they were winning. But when Moses' arms grew weary and the banner dropped below their vision, they began to lose. It was the banner of the Lord that reminded them who they were and encouraged them to give with all the gusto and courage they had.

I am beginning to realize that I need to lift my eyes up from the valley a little more frequently these days and recall the "banner of the Lord" and why we are here, what we are supposed to be about. God is at the TOP of the list. That is the only way we are able to make it through any of the valleys of life and come out on the other side better, stronger, and fit for the next place to which God calls us—even if it is back to the same place.

In our conference, it may not be a coincidence that the appointment season begins just about the same time as Lent each year. Perhaps it is no mistake that we are called to a time of repentance and self-denial as the first phone calls are made—calls that ask us (churches and pastors alike) to step up to a higher standard, to be held accountable for measurable, intentional growth.

Formed in a Spirit of Generosity

My daddy's real name was Melvin, but most of his friends called him Mike. Melvin is a pretty old-fashioned name, even for my dad's era. Melvin Olaf Olson. Please, let us be clear, that's O-L-S-O-N. It's Norwegian, not Swedish. As a young boy my grandfather emigrated from Norway to the United States. I am very proud to be the daughter of Melvin Olaf Olson. Daddy was the kind of fellow who would give someone the shirt off his back. I have literally seen him do so—and more.

When I was in high school we lived in a town east of Austin. In his later years Daddy worked at Brackenridge Hospital in downtown Austin. He worked with a wonderful man named Luna. Mr. Luna (as I called him) and his wife had ten children. Luna was in a terrible car accident and totaled his car. So for at least two years that I remember, every morning my dad drove from our house, twenty-plus miles to the east, picked up Mr. Luna, and then they drove back to Austin to work together. In the evening they reversed the process. That's more than eighty miles a day and about an hour and a half my dad drove out of his way to go pick up a coworker. Eventually Daddy convinced my mom they could afford a new truck for Dad to drive and Daddy gave Mr. Luna his truck.

My dad was a remarkable man. There is a reason for it.

I am thankful to not know the details, but I do remember hearing stories about how my grandfather would pummel my dad when Daddy was a boy. Not with a spanking—with his fists. So it is really not much of a surprise to me that when my dad was about seven or eight years old he found First Lutheran Church of Northwood, Iowa. He started by going to Vacation Bible School one summer. Are you paying attention, VBS teachers? This boy whose father had literally beaten the snot out of him gained entry to the church through Vacation Bible School. After that, Daddy got himself up on Sunday mornings and walked to church. I don't know how long he did that, but I do know it was reported to be a long time—a very long time. Eventually he was baptized and confirmed in the First Lutheran Church. I proudly display that portrait in my living room.

One day Daddy went home from church and Sunday school, and I suspect his gait was a little different—determined, intentional. He walked straight up to my four-foot-eight-inch grandmother and said, "Ma! Ma! Did you know you're a *heathen*? Ma, if you don't start going to church, you're goin' straight to hell!" John the Baptist or Billy Graham didn't have anything on my dad! My grandmother started going to church with him the very next Sunday. She went to church the rest of her life.

The work of those early VBS days, Sunday school, and high liturgical worship carried my dad through a lifetime of tumult.

82

They formed him into the kind of person who would drive eighty miles on a daily basis to get a friend to work and then give him his pickup truck. Why? Because ultimately Daddy knew he was God's child. He knew because of people like you that God had named him and claimed him and made him God's own.

When we know—really know—that we are God's children, it makes a tangible difference in the way we live our lives. When a child is delivered from the fists of an angry man and delivered into the arms of the mother church, that child is a changed child— for life. That doesn't mean he grows up to be perfect. It does mean he has the possibility of growing up to be better than the previous generation.

We have a lot of opportunity, Church!

Daddy was caught by the love of God! It was my daddy's love, imperfections and all, that set an example and led the way for me to be caught. Once we are really caught, we love to fish. We love fishing so much that we are willing to spend the rest of our lives fishing off a dock or in a marina; off jetties and standing on piers; at home or away. We fish early in the morning or late into the night, in deep and in shallow water. Once we are caught, there is just nothing better than fishing and catching fish for the One who calls us to throw our nets on the other side of the boat, far into the deep water.

Chapter 7

Relationship to the Source of All Life

Blessed are those who trust in the LORD,
whose trust is the LORD.
They shall be like a tree planted by water,
sending out its roots by the stream.
It shall not fear when heat comes,
and its leaves shall stay green;
in the year of drought it is not anxious,
and it does not cease to bear fruit.

—Jeremiah 17:7-8

Planting Something New

There was a pastor who was known for the gorgeous rose garden he grew at the church. Roses of all different colors and varieties surrounded the church. That pastor was a master rose gardener. The church loved him. He loved the church. Everybody was happy—at least in that era. The church was renowned for the beauty of its roses and their fragrance. All the neighbors who moved into the area—of which there were many—admired the church with the rose gardens on their way past.

Years after the pastor left the church, the traffic around the church with the rose gardens grew. The traffic became more harried. The pollution grew worse. A highway was built right next to the church of roses. The roses began to wilt from the smog as the people rushed by.

Soon the elected officers of the congregation looked around and noticed that nobody tended the roses anymore. The leaves on the bushes were spotted, and the branches needed pruning. Not only that, the people didn't seem to care much about the roses anymore. As a matter of fact, the people didn't seem to care much for anything anymore—that is, anything except for those people who were inside the church.

They held potlucks. They paid for the youth to go on ski trips. They held a Lord's Acre and had a silent auction to pay their apportionments. One by one the members inside that congregation, like the roses outside, began to lose their petals. Eventually they grew brittle and began to lose their sap. Like untended roses, they too began to pass away. One day the leaders of the church began to realize their beloved church was dying. They started asking one another questions—hard questions. They began to wrestle with answers that were not easy. They struggled between holding on to the way things had always been and digging up those rose bushes and planting something new.

For Just Such a Time as This

In the fourth chapter of the book of Esther, Mordecai holds Esther accountable to her people, to her heritage, and to her call. "Who knows? Perhaps you have come to royal dignity for just such a time as this," he says. I *hear*, "Esther, you have a responsibility. Whether you like it or not, *you have a job to do.*"

By virtue of you reading this book, Mordecai speaks. There is work to be done. God is calling us, whether we like it or not, into responsibility and accountability for that work.

The middle-aged couple had more than just a few gray hairs on their heads. Life had not been easy or kind to them. They had been together through sixteen years of marriage—every single one lived week to week, paycheck to paycheck. Three—now four—children plus a combined total of eight miscarriages and stillbirths had stacked medical bills almost higher than they could see. The woman was not in good health—mentally, physically, or emotionally.

They were moving to Texas hoping to find a fresh start, praying that the hot air and drier climate would provide relief from the harsh Iowa winters and would help the woman's physical ailments. They were afraid. It was one more attempt to stretch far enough to make it to the promised land—whatever that was.

And then the baby—the new baby girl, born premature to a couple who was long overdue such a child—got pneumonia. It was not only pneumonia; it was double pneumonia. Both lungs were full of thick fluid. She fought for each rattling breath. One night as that middle-aged, graying couple sat on the edge of their bed, they held her, listening to her rattle, and they prayed. I don't know exactly what the prayer said, but I do know it went something like this:

Dear God, we have had so much loss—eight babies. The children need shoes, and the pantry is empty. But right now, God, we pray for this tiny baby. God, we have wanted her every bit as much as we wanted the others. Please, Lord, don't let her die. She is your child. We give her to you. And if you will just let her live, we promise to dedicate her life to you. Let her live, God. Let her live.

They lifted the baby up. Her breathing eased a bit. And they went on with life.

It took about thirty-five years for that covenant between my parents and God to be fulfilled. When I was thirty and told my mom I was going into the ordained ministry, she tried to renege on the prayer. She said to me, "It is my duty and obligation as your mother to tell you that if you go into the ordained ministry then you are abandoning your husband and making orphans of your children." I think she had forgotten her prayer! But God had not!

For thirty years I ran in the opposite direction from God. I believe God would have allowed me to continue running too, if that is what I had chosen to do. But there was something nagging, begging, and pleading inside of me. Why did God call me? I have no idea. Perhaps it was the same reason God called you—laity and clergy alike—for just such a time as this.

To what is God calling us? For what has God created us? What gifts and graces is God calling us to use for the building up and for the salvation of all God's people? Is it to tend roses? Or has God called us for a different time—for a time such as this?

Ground Cover

A lot of ground has been covered in the preceding chapters. There have been a lot of words written about relationships and change. It is all a bunch of useless garble unless you and I realize that God has called us to make a difference in this world—here and now. God has called us to this time and this place to lead our churches and all God's people into a new day. God has called us into new relationships with God and with one another. God may be asking more of us than we had ever realized and certainly more than we have bargained for.

Ronald Heifetz, Alexander Grashow, and Marty Linsky remind us: "The word *leader* comes from the Indo-European root word *leit*, the name for the person who carried the flag in front of an army going into battle and usually died in the first enemy attack. His sacrifice would alert the rest of the army to the location of the danger ahead."[1] Does that mean God is calling us to give and give and give until we are completely "given out"? No! Does it mean that God is calling us to give our very lives? Absolutely yes! God will not leave us; God will not abandon or forsake us. We can stake our lives on it!

Relevance for This Age

One of the wonderful women with whom I became friends years ago told a story about her daughter who is hearing impaired but who with the assistance of hearing aids is able to function extremely well. Like many people who have a hearing deficit, sometimes her daughter doesn't realize how loudly she is speaking.

My friend and her family participated in the life of a large church that had a vast and acoustically live sanctuary. One time the family was sitting in worship together and the priest was giving the sermon. He was droning on and on. He was reading from the page, head down, in an incredibly monotonous voice. My friend's daughter, who was eight or nine at the time, had had just about all she could take of the dreadful sermon. The priest paused to take a deep breath, and at just about that time, the daughter blurted out in a voice much louder than she intended, and much louder than her mother would ever have desired, "This is so boring!" It literally echoed in the sanctuary.

The congregation laughed. The priest did not.

Do you ever get bored with worship? How many of our children, youth, and young adults get bored with worship? Look around. How many of them do you see in your church? Let me ask it another way: do you speak the predominant language of the culture?

Social Media

Ten years ago, five years ago, even three years ago I would never have believed you if you had told me that I would be sitting at my desk in Weatherford, Texas, coaching our son, who is in Austin, on how to best sit by his only surviving grandfather to help him pass from this world into the next—all via text message! But that is the primary way I spent a morning late last October. I shared the deep parts of my soul via text with a twenty-five-year-old young man, to help him know how to best mediate, how to best share the love of Christ at a critical time.

Our world is changing—and it is changing fast. The words that I have heard that bring some of the deepest, most intense sorrow to my heart during this season of change have been something like this, "Those people should be involved in church. We are doing all we can to help them see they need to join us. Why wouldn't anyone want to be a part of what we are doing? We're a loving, friendly church! We've been here for decades; all they have to do is walk in the door!"

Oh, my. Do you hear the hegemony in those words? Every time one new person enters our sanctuaries or joins our congregations, we have an opportunity to be made brand-new. Like the stories in previous chapters, it is our responsibility to step out of our comfort zone and meet people where they are.

What Is Required

Before our Lord was anointed with oil and betrayed into the hands of soldiers, he told the parable commonly known as the sheep and the goats (Matt. 25:31-46). The King judges the people of the nations, and they are separated into those on the right and those on the left. One group has taken care of those in need; the other has not. As the Gospel writer of Matthew is apt to say, those who do not do as our Lord has desired will be sent away with wailing and gnashing of teeth.

Sometimes I wonder, is that gnashing of teeth due to the sheer recognition that we did not do what our Lord required of us and then living with the knowledge deep in our souls that we let God down? I can't imagine any punishment more anguishing than to know that God was depending on me and I blew it. I can't imagine any grace more saving than to know that I blew it and God chooses to love me—to love you—anyway! Not only that, God chooses to take away the anguish of me knowing that I blew it. Wow! *That* is grace!

Christ is the One who makes that grace possible. Christ is our mediator—our go-between. Out of our response, we too should then be a "go-between" kind of people. As Christians we are called to be the people who help those who don't know God, connect to God.

Jesus didn't say, "Come on over to Nazareth, and I'll share my story about God with you." Jesus went out. Jesus went to places where people were hurting; where there was need; where people were hungry to hear the word. In fact, I really believe that if text messaging had been a known means of communication in Jesus' day, he would have had thumbs that moved at lightning speed! I believe Jesus would have used multimedia in worship. (He *did* use kinesthetic means of teaching—tangible things like water, bread, fish, nets, mud, fig trees, and so on.) I don't think Jesus would have cared what kind of music was sung or what tunes were used as long as the music gave God honor and glory and mediated God's grace.

Where did we get the idea that we could sit in our pews and that people had to come through the doors to learn about God? My brothers and sisters in Christ, we simply must—for the sake of Jesus Christ—learn a new way to do and to be church! We must go out!

Mediating God

That is why I am very excited about the opportunity to be in ministry in this season of life. I see more opportunity before us than I have ever seen before. We have the blessed, sacred choice of mediating the grace of God in ways that have never before been tried. Isn't that cool? Like text messaging a young man and coaching him on how to hold the hand of an old man who is dying, you and I stand in the gap between what is known and what is unknown, what is seen and what is unseen.

A Mighty Fortress

Sometimes legends become such a part of the fabric of who we are that we can't distinguish fact from fiction. Maybe legend, but I believe fact, is the notion that Martin Luther used the tunes from the barrooms of his day, put Christian words to the melody, and used the songs for teaching the faith. It was said that "A Mighty Fortress Is Our God" began as a rousing bar tune.

Stop and think about that for just a moment. We often think the Church is to be a fortress. In Luther's hymn it is God who is the fortress. The Church has the role of mediating God to a world that does not know God. The means of communicating that message is the melody of the world—not of the Church.

How would worship change if we did the same? What if we met people where they are, and rather than trying to convince, coerce, and cajole them into doing things our way, we met them on their terms? Instead of balking at the use of multimedia, contemporary worship, and visual and kinesthetic aids in worship, why not use them to convey good theology to a contemporary culture? Are we willing to do whatever it takes to communicate the message God has given us to share?

My Soul Magnifies the Lord

In Luke 1:46-47 Mary said, "My soul magnifies the Lord, and my spirit rejoices in God my Savior." There are times, places, events, and even people who magnify God—who help us see God more clearly—and they make God look bigger than we had ever realized God could be. Mary's soul magnified God—and God looked bigger to the rest of us because of her. Blessed is she who reveals the Lord!

I remember as a child sitting out in front of Wanda's house with her son Mark. Mark had the most incredible thing. I'd never seen one before. He called it a magnifier. I sat on my haunches and watched with wonder as Mark revealed the miracles of a magnifier. When I looked through it, I could see the little, tiny capillaries that carried nutrition out to the tips of a sycamore leaf. I could see the hair on Mark's face (which was pretty amazing considering he was about six at the time). It was astonishing!

Then Mark did the most magical thing. He took that magnifier, positioned it just right with the sun shining through, and focused the light on the center of the sycamore leaf. Within moments the leaf began to smolder and then POOF! It ignited into flames. I was aghast! Then there was this little caterpillar. Nah—I don't think I'll tell you about the caterpillar!

Have you ever been amazed by the power of a magnifier (or, as most people call it, a magnifying glass)? Do you remember looking at the curvature of the lens, wondering how scientists thought up such a scheme? If you wear bifocals (like me) there is no doubt about the benefits of a magnifier. Life looks completely different when you can see—or when you can't!

It was thrilling to be interviewed by the press for a national story they did on various perspectives of Christmas. One question the reporter asked me was about the virgin birth and if I really believed it was so. I was caught a little off guard but found myself saying to him, "Do I believe that God is a big enough God that God could cause Mary to immaculately conceive and bear the Son of God in her womb? You bet I do!"

Then I thought for a moment and continued, "But for me the real question is, do I believe God is big enough that God can be born in me—and in each of us? That God can instill in each of us a sense of God's self that is so tangible that Christ can be born into the world *through us*?" That is the real question for me. And even more, the personal question I must ask myself is, "Does my soul make God look bigger to the rest of the world? Will I bear Christ in the world by allowing Christ to live in me and through me in such a way that the presence of God is undeniable?"

The first step of that journey begins with doing the best we can—right where we are. When will we realize that nothing is impossible with God? God's design is for us to respond, like Mary, "Here am I, the servant of the Lord," so that our lives are the fulfillment of what God has promised.

Mary gave of her best. She did her part. She did what she could. And her soul magnified the Lord. Perhaps we could even hear her invite us from Psalm 34:1-3:

I will bless the LORD at all times;
    his praise shall continually be in my mouth.

My soul makes its boast in the LORD;
>   let the humble hear and be glad.
O magnify the LORD with me,
>   and let us exalt his name together.

Rooted by Living Waters

Traveling through Israel and Palestine is a theological feast. I vividly remember the utter desolation of the land surrounding the Dead Sea—rocks. There were big rocks, little rocks, and ground-up rocks called sand or dirt; not much else, just rocks. Jeremiah 17:5-8 speaks of those who metaphorically live in such a land. We live there because we depend on our own abilities, because our own flesh is our strength. Our hearts are turned away from God. In verse six we hear:

They shall be like a shrub in the desert,
>   and shall not see when relief comes.
They shall live in the parched places of the wilderness,
>   in an uninhabited salt land.

Exile—that's what Jeremiah is talking about. Exile. Being completely cut off. The shrubs in the desert aren't even watered by rain. The rocks and dirt are so hard that when the rains come—they come in a downpour—the water doesn't soak in. It just runs down those rocky hillsides and into a wadi—a dry riverbed—and ultimately into the Dead Sea.

Listen to the next verses, 7-8:

Blessed are those who trust in the LORD,
>   whose trust is the LORD.
They shall be like a tree planted by water,
>   sending out its roots by the stream.
It shall not fear when heat comes,
>   and its leaves shall stay green;
in the year of drought it is not anxious,
>   and it does not cease to bear fruit.

"They shall be like a tree planted by water." The word *planted* in Hebrew doesn't just mean "planted"; it means "transplanted."[2] "Blessed are those who trust in the LORD, whose trust is the LORD.

They shall be like a tree *transplanted* by water." That tree is plucked up out of the arid, lifeless desert. It is carefully dug up; the roots are gently and cautiously moved; and then it is transplanted. Imagine, it isn't moved just a little, but hundreds of miles north to Galilee. It is transplanted smack in the middle of that fertile basin, right next to the living water of God, and it puts down deep roots into rich soil. The bush that was once dying of thirst grows in stature, standing tall. Rocks and salt no longer bind the weary bush. It branches into a tree that blossoms and bears fruit because its roots have access to living water. It is no longer alone in a dry and weary land!

Could it be that God is working to transplant and transform us? Of course it could be so! All transplants require some sort of disruption, pruning, and risk. When we are full of apprehension, anxiety, and fear, God reminds us that a transplanted tree need not fear when the weather is hot; it need not be anxious when the drought comes.

Church! We are planted by living waters. We too have no reason to fear or to be anxious if we are allowing God to move us to new places, because the best is yet to come.

I Know That My Redeemer Lives

When our daughter Erin was three years old, I went back to work and put Erin and Matthew into day care. One morning as we were about to rush out the door, late as usual, she came and told me that her hamster was sick. I went to look, and sure enough, it was really sick. In fact, there was no doubt about it; it was dying. Well, what does one do with a dying hamster and a three-year-old? Since I was already late for work, I did the only thing I could do. I found a plastic seal-tight container, put the hamster in it, and broke the news, "Erin, honey, your hamster is dead."

I don't know what I expected, but she burst into tears. I tried to console her, but I was now really late for work, and so as tenderly as I could, I said, "Erin, what do you want to do? Do you want to wait until this evening, and then we can have a funeral and bury your hamster?"

With the back of her hand slung across her forehead, my precious three-year-old exclaimed, "I don't know! I just *can't deal* with this right now!"

Somehow, we managed to get to day care and to work that day.

Later that evening, when we got home from day care, I waited a while and then said ever so gently, "Erin, honey, your hamster is going to start to smell. It's still in the plastic dish on the dryer. What do you want to do with it?" Squatting down and hugging her, I asked, "Honey, do you want to have a funeral for it?"

"Oh, Mom!" she replied (with her hands on her hips this time). "Throw it out in the pasture, flush it down the toilet, feed it to the dog; it doesn't matter—the darn thing is dead!"

Well, dead *is* dead—and even a three-year-old knows the difference!

AND WE ARE NOT DEAD!

Listen, Church! We believe in God. We believe in Jesus Christ. Jesus didn't just have a blackout. Christ died dead! That is why we extinguish the candle on Good Friday. Dead is dead. On the third day God proved God was victorious over death and raised Christ, not resuscitated him. God raised Christ up from the dead! We believe in the Holy Spirit, who abides with us now and forever. We believe that God has not, God will not—not now, not ever—abandon us or forsake us!

Do you believe that?

Do we live like it?

Lord, I love the Church! She is that magnificent place where you stand in the gap between your kingdom in heaven and your kingdom on earth. Sometimes she is broken and brokenhearted. Sometimes she is the reason that people are able to see you face-to-face.

Lord, we love the Church! And we want to be a part of your kingdom that is alive here and now, in this world and in the world to come. We want to be mediators of your grace and of your glory. Equip us. Empower us. Give us eyes that see, hearts that are on fire, and hands that can't help but serve you. Come, Almighty God! We need your help!

Notes

Introduction: Rigorous Relationships and Why They Matter

1. L. Gregory Jones and Susan Jones, "Pivotal Leadership," *Christian Century* 118, no. 25 (2001): 24–29.

2. Kobi Yamada, *Ever Wonder: Ask Questions and Live into the Answers* (Seattle: Compendium, 2008).

3. Arthur P. Bochner and Carol S. Ellis, "Which Way to Turn?" *Journal of Contemporary Ethnography* 28, no. 5 (1999): 493.

4. Arthur P. Bochner, "It's about Time: Narrative and the Divided Self," *Qualitative Inquiry* 3, no. 4 (1997): 418–38.

5. Margaret J. Wheatley, *Finding Our Way: Leadership for an Uncertain Time* (San Francisco: Berrett-Koehler, 2005; 2007).

6. Margaret J. Wheatley, *Leadership and the New Science: Discovering Order in a Chaotic World*, 3rd ed. (San Francisco: Berrett-Koehler, 2006).

7. Ibid., 39.

1. In the Beginning GOD: Relationships with God and God's People

1. The Reverend Dick Murray taught Christian Education courses at Perkins School of Theology, Southern Methodist University, Dallas. He was instrumental in the development of the DISCIPLE Bible Study. In addition, he taught workshops at the local church level. I was blessed to learn from him in all three settings.

2. Margaret J. Wheatley, *Turning to One Another: Simple Conversations to Restore Hope to the Future* (San Francisco: Berrett-Koehler, 2002), 47.

3. Parker J. Palmer, *Let Your Life Speak: Listening for the Voice of Vocation* (San Francisco: Jossey-Bass, 2000), 16.

4. Ibid., 17.

5. Ibid., 32.

6. Ibid., 32–33.

7. Albert C. Outler and Richard P. Heitzenrater, *John Wesley's Sermons: An Anthology* (Nashville: Abingdon Press, 1991).

8. Wheatley, *Turning to One Another.*

9. Ibid., 98.

10. Peter F. Drucker, *The Effective Executive* (New York: HarperBusiness, 1993).

11. Linda Lantieri, *Building Emotional Intelligence: Techniques to Cultivate Inner Strength in Children* (Boulder: Sounds True, 2008).

12. Ronald A. Heifetz and Marty Linsky, *Leadership on the Line: Staying Alive through the Dangers of Leading* (Boston: Harvard Business School Press, 2002).

2. Relationships of Accountability, Support, Trust, and Integrity

1. Pepper Choplin, "Wake Up, Church, Wake Up!" Copyright © 2003 by the Lorenz Publishing Company.

2. L. Gregory Jones and Kevin R. Armstrong, *Resurrecting Excellence: Shaping Faithful Christian Ministry* (Grand Rapids: Eerdmans, 2006), 76.

3. Ibid., 78.

4. Peter F. Drucker, *The Effective Executive* (New York: HarperBusiness, 1993), 58.

5. Stephen M. R. Covey, *The Speed of Trust: The One Thing That Changes Everything* (New York: Free Press, 2006), 30.

6. Ibid., 138.

7. Margaret J. Wheatley, *Turning to One Another: Simple Conversations to Restore Hope to the Future* (San Francisco: Berrett-Koehler, 2002), 141.

8. Covey, *The Speed of Trust*, 138–39.

9. The Arbinger Institute; *Leadership and Self-Deception* (San Francisco: Berrett-Koehler, 2000; 2002), 106.

10. Covey, *The Speed of Trust*, 303–4.

11. Robert E. Quinn, *Deep Change: Discovering the Leader Within* (San Francisco: Jossey-Bass, 1996), 19.

12. Dean Williams, *Real Leadership: Helping People and Organizations Face Their Toughest Challenges* (San Francisco: Berrett-Koehler, 2005), 243.

3. Relationships with Those around Us

1. Virginia O. Bassford, "Perspectives of Strength: Female Elders in United Methodist Ministry" (PhD diss., Texas Woman's University, 2008).

2. Michael E. Kerr and Murray Bowen, *Family Evaluation: An Approach Based on Bowen Theory* (New York: W. W. Norton, 1988).

3. Ibid., ix. Core concepts in Bowen theory are emotional systems, pressure to adapt in order to keep individuality and togetherness stabilized, self-differentiation, triangulation, and anxiety.

4. For more information on the *Call to Action*, please see http://www.umc.org/site/c.lwL4KnN1LtH/b.5792195/k.BDBE/Call_to_Action_Reordering_the_Life_of_the_Church.htm

5. Phyllis Tickle, *The Great Emergence: How Christianity Is Changing and Why* (Grand Rapids: Baker Books, 2008), 27.

6. The Appalachia Service Project began as a ministry of The United Methodist Church. For more information, please see http://asphome.org/. ASP is the ministry after which the Central Texas Conference Youth in Mission (CTCYM) program was patterned when I wrote the first curriculum and organized it in 1993–94 so home repairs could be done after the great floods of 1993 in the Midwest. ASP utilizes high school youth and adult volunteers to facilitate nine weeks of home repair and reconstruction in the Appalachian areas of Virginia, West Virginia, Kentucky, North Carolina, and Tennessee.

7. Richard E. Stearns, *The Hole in Our Gospel* (Nashville: Thomas Nelson, 2009), 59.

8. *The Theological Dictionary of the New Testament*, ed. and trans. Geoffrey W. Bromiley (Grand Rapids: Eerdmans, 1965).

9. Albert Outler and Richard P. Heitzenrater, *John Wesley's Sermons: An Anthology* (Nashville: Abingdon Press, 1991), 490.

4. Relationships with the Unexpected and Burnout

1. See http://www.theexplodingwhale.com.

2. Margaret J. Wheatley, *Leadership and the New Science: Discovering Order in a Chaotic World*, 3rd ed. (San Francisco: Berrett-Koehler, 2006), 78.

3. Ibid., 21.

4. Ronald A. Heifetz and Marty Linsky, *Leadership on the Line: Staying Alive through the Dangers of Leading.* (Boston: Harvard Business School Press, 2001), 142.

5. Margaret J. Wheatley, *Finding Our Way: Leadership for an Uncertain Time* (San Francisco: Berrett-Koehler, 2005; 2007).

6. Emmy E. Werner and Ruth S. Smith, *Journeys from Childhood to Midlife: Risk, Resilience, and Recovery* (Ithaca, NY: Cornell University Press, 2001).

7. Ibid.

8. See Froma Walsh, *Strengthening Family Resilience* (New York: Guilford Press, 1998).

9. D. L. Coutu, "How Resilience Works," *Harvard Business Review* 80, no. 5 (2002): 46–55.

10. See also Christina Maslach, *Burnout: The Cost of Caring* (Cambridge, MA: Malor Books, 2003.

11. Edwin H. Friedman, *A Failure of Nerve: Leadership in the Age of the Quick Fix* (Bethesda, MD: The Friedman Estate, 1999), 256.

12. Ibid., 22.

13. Christina Maslach and Michael P. Leiter, *The Truth about Burnout: How Organizations Cause Personal Stress and What to Do about It* (San Francisco: Jossey-Bass, 1997), 24.

14. Ibid., 18.

15. Christina Maslach, "What Have We Learned about Burnout and Health?" *Psychology and Health* 16, no. 5 (2001): 610.

16. Friedman, *A Failure of Nerve*, 256.

17. Parker J. Palmer, *Let Your Life Speak: Listening for the Voice of Vocation* (San Francisco: Jossey-Bass, 2000), 49.

5. Relationship to Leadership and a Future with Hope

1. Ronald Heifetz and Marty Linsky are creative, gifted, and empowering teachers. Their teaching methodology is vast, and their ability to adapt to the learner is adept. To learn more about the courses they teach, see the programs listed at: http://ksgexecprogram.harvard.edu/

2. See Margaret J. Wheatley, *Leadership and the New Science: Discovering Order in a Chaotic World*, 3rd ed. (San Francisco: Berrett-Koehler, 2006); *Finding Our Way:*

Leadership for an Uncertain Time (San Francisco: Berrett-Koehler, 2005); and *Turning to One Another: Simple Conversations to Restore Hope to the Future* (San Francisco: Berrett-Koehler, 2002).

3. Daniel Goleman, *Emotional Intelligence* (New York: Bantam, 1994).

4. Ronald A. Heifetz, *Leadership without Easy Answers* (Cambridge, MA: Belknap Press of Harvard University Press, 1994), 250–76.

5. Ibid., 252–63.

6. Ibid., 268.

7. Ibid., 269.

8. Ibid., 273.

9. Ronald A. Heifetz, Alexander Grashow, and Marty Linsky, *The Practice of Adaptive Leadership: Tools and Tactics for Changing Your Organization and the World* (Boston: Harvard Business Press, 2009), 14. Italics are as in the original.

10. Ronald A. Heifetz uses the balcony metaphor in several of his works.

11. Ronald A. Heifetz and Marty Linsky, *Leadership on the Line: Staying Alive through the Dangers of Leading* (Boston: Harvard Business Press, 2002), 117.

12. D. L. Coutu, "The Anxiety of Learning," *Harvard Business Review* 80, no. 3 (2002): 1–8.

13. Heifetz and Linsky, *Leadership on the Line*, 117.

14. Tony Wagner, *The Global Achievement Gap: Why Even Our Best Schools Don't Teach the New Survival Skills Our Children Need—and What We Can Do about It* (New York: Basic Books, 2008). Other, similar works can be found on Wagner's website: http://www.tonywagner.com.

15. P. Clampitt, M. L. Williams, and R. J. DeKoch, "Embracing Uncertainty: The Executive's Challenge," *Journal of Change Management* 2, no. 3 (2002): 212–28.

16. D. Miller, "Successful Change Leaders: What Makes Them? What Do They Do That Is Different?" *Journal of Change Management* 2, no. 4 (2002): 359.

17. Margaret J. Wheatley, *Leadership and the New Science: Discovering Order in a Chaotic World*, 3rd ed. (San Francisco: Berrett-Koehler, 2006), 102.

18. Heifetz, Grashow, and Linsky, *The Practice of Adaptive Leadership*, 126–32.

19. Margaret J. Wheatley, *Finding Our Way: Leadership for an Uncertain Time* (San Francisco: Berrett-Koehler, 2005), 70.

20. "The Force" Volkswagen commercial. Retrieved from: http://www.youtube.com/watch?v=R55e-uHQna0

21. John Bowring, "In the Cross of Christ I Glory," 1825.

22. Virginia O. Bassford, "Perspectives of Strength: Female Elders in United Methodist Ministry" (PhD diss., Texas Woman's University, 2008).

23. Heifetz, Grashow, and Linsky, *The Practice of Adaptive Leadership*, 20.

24. This is a phrase that our cabinet first used in utter exhaustion. It has become a catchphrase for going round in circles.

25. Heifetz and Linsky, *Leadership on the Line*, 20.

26. Heifetz, Grashow, and Linsky, *The Practice of Adaptive Leadership*.

27. The translation of the Hebrew text found in Exodus 3:7b is, "Indeed, I have *experienced* their sufferings." The NRSV translates the word *yatha* as "know," which is not a head knowledge, but rather a knowledge because God has been with them and has experienced the suffering with the Children of Israel.

6. Relationship to the Vocation of Ministry and Full-time Christian Service

1. Kenda Creasy Dean, *Almost Christian: What the Faith of Our Teenagers Is Telling the American Church* (New York: Oxford University Press, 2010), 4.

2. Tony Wagner, *The Global Achievement Gap: Why Even Our Best Schools Don't Teach the New Survival Skills Our Children Need—and What We Can Do about It* (New York: Basic Books, 2008), 140.

3. Ibid., 156.

4. Ibid., 164.

5. Ronald A. Heifetz and Marty Linsky, *Leadership on the Line: Staying Alive through the Dangers of Leading* (Boston: Harvard Business School Press, 2002), 14.

6. Margaret J. Wheatley, *Leadership and the New Science: Discovering Order in a Chaotic World*, 3rd ed. (San Francisco: Berrett-Koehler, 2006), 99.

7. Relationship to the Source of All Life

1. Ronald A. Heifetz, Alexander Grashow, Marty Linsky, *The Practice of Adaptive Leadership: Tools and Tactics for Changing Your Organization and the World* (Boston: Harvard Business Press, 2009), 26.

2. *The New Interpreter's Bible: A Commentary in Twelve Volumes*, vol. 4 (Nashville: Abingdon Press, 2001).

CPSIA information can be obtained at www.ICGtesting.com
Printed in the USA
LVOW080154221211

260575LV00004B/3/P